Arcane Arts

The Dungeoneer's Guide to Miniature Painting and Tabletop Mayhem

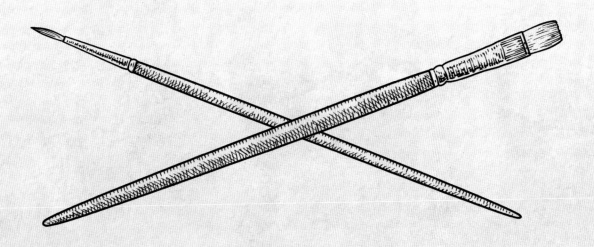

Andrews McMeel Publishing
a division of Andrews McMeel Universal
1130 Walnut Street, Kansas City, Missouri 64106

www.andrewsmcmeel.com

22 23 24 25 26 SHO 10 9 8 7 6 5 4 3 2 1

ISBN: 978-1-5248-6373-9

Library of Congress Control Number: 2022937223

Editor: Katie Gould
Art Director: Holly Swayne
Designer: Sierra S. Stanton
Production Editor: Jasmine Lim
Production Manager: Tamara Haus

ATTENTION: SCHOOLS AND BUSINESSES

Andrews McMeel books are available at quantity discounts with bulk purchase for educational, business, or sales promotional use. For information, please e-mail the Andrews McMeel Publishing Special Sales Department: specialsales@amuniversal.com.

Arcane Arts

THE DUNGEONEER'S GUIDE TO MINIATURE PAINTING AND TABLETOP MAYHEM

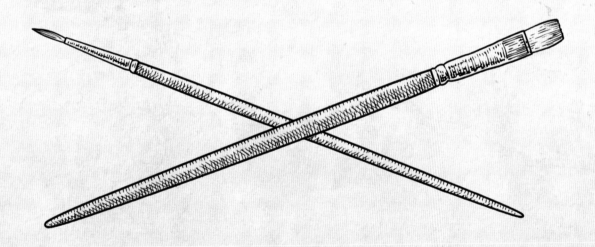

Noxweiler Ignatius Berf

Andrews McMeel
PUBLISHING®

Table of Contents

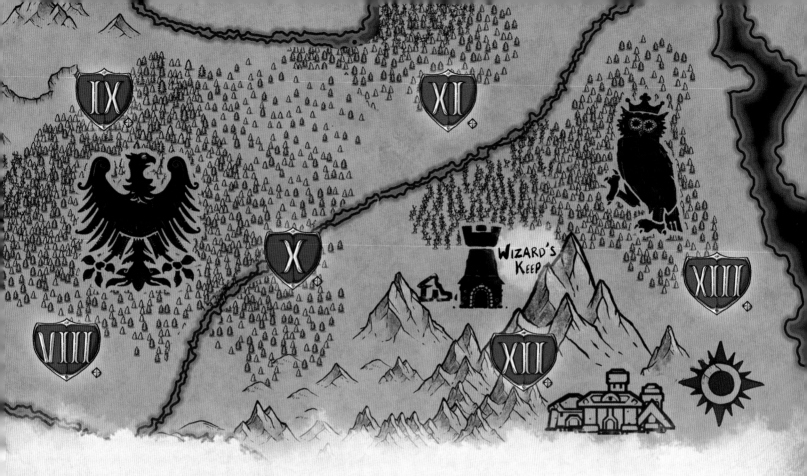

It cannot be overstated, dear friend, that every journey—before it is undertaken—can be both daunting and exhilarating. Whether you are prepared or not, your destination awaits and beckons you onward; your memories of moments past may be neatly packed up and carried upon your back, but the rest must be left behind as you venture forth.

Those who quit the road may return home, but they are never really the same as when they left, and who is to say that their true destination was left undiscovered.

Forgive me. Where are my manners? I suppose that I've been out here in the wilderness too long . . . crawling through the dank and dangerous dungeons of the many realms. My chosen profession is academic in nature, but—here—I'll be serving you as a guide.

While it is not for everyone, if you have a penchant for adventure and a thirst for knowledge and artistic discovery, I'd be happy to show you the way. In fact, I believe that I have a map that can direct you to a—thankfully—empty dragon's lair that would be perfect for you to cut your adventuring teeth on.

If you are ready to make your way into a fantastic world filled with wonders untold, gather your supplies, study the map that I've enclosed in the journal that you hold in your hands, and allow yourself to get lost in imagination and creativity. It doesn't take much effort, just call upon that part of yourself that spent long summer days chasing invisible faeries and digging for buried treasure in your neighbor's garden.

It isn't hard to remember the magic that you used to wield, and I hope that these Quests and tales help show you the way.

Well, friend, we should get moving; there is a bugbear that followed me through the last Gateway and I really don't wish to face them without a sizable sack of gold coins to replace the one that I borrowed to placate the minotaur near Quest 13.

In Paint and Adventure,

Maxweiler Ignatius Benton

Your Guide through the Many Realms, Designer of Dungeons, Sometimes Artist, Eternal Dreamer

Introduction

Having retrieved the ancient scroll case from the strange old man that sat at the hearth of the tavern known as the Wandering Wyvern, you make your way back into the bustling and chaotic streets of the city. Carriages and horseback riders travel up and down the cobblestone roads carrying passengers and goods to destinations throughout the realms. You have paid good coin for the map that is contained within that tattered, leather scroll case—everything that you had to your name, truth be told.

You stand, ready to embark on your first adventure, and every great adventure begins with a single step. And every great adventurer needs a map. Consider the book that you hold in your hands to be yours.

The destination, however, is entirely up to you.

This book is an anomaly; it straddles the line between truth and fable, instruction and fancy, utility and novelty. Much like the imaginative and vast hobby of fantasy tabletop miniature painting and crafting, these instructions ask you to feed the fire of your creative spirit and explore worlds of your own creation. Using three levels of instruction, with exercises and challenges that are split into Quests, this book will provide you with the tools necessary to become a better hobbyist, painter, and crafter.

If you are a new or avid player of tabletop roleplaying games, miniature war-games, and other such endeavors, then you may be quite familiar with the process of creating the necessary characters and settings, people and places, dragons and dungeons, castles, cabins, and cottages of a thousand upon thousand imagined realms. If that is how you found yourself here, or if you are a hobby painter seeking new inspiration, I welcome you to the exciting endeavor of transforming your pen and paper encounters into an immersive event that brings the gravitas of your full imagination directly onto your tabletop!

This book will help you to create and embellish countless worlds of imagination!

I, quite humbly, invite you to join me as we work together to both improve your skills and ignite your inspiration! This hobby is a bridge to the countless wonders of your imagination, and no skill or technique that I can teach you will ever surpass the wellspring of creativity that already exists within you. I encourage you to exercise your ability to believe in the impossible as well as your ability to blend, stipple, and layer paint.

Shall we begin?

Welcome to the Adventurer's Guild

With the intention of undertaking the rewarding hobby of miniature painting, other than your eagerness and willingness to learn, you will need a selection of materials and the knowledge on how to safely handle the varied tools of your chosen craft. It can be daunting, perhaps even intimidating, to look across the sea of brushes and paints, knives and files, glues and putties, and to make choices that you feel are right for the specific projects that you have set before yourself. Never fear, before we send you off on your first Quests, I—and my friend **Thaco Thistle-Britches**—are going to ensure that you are properly outfitted and instructed on the tools that you will wield and the way in which to use them safely and confidently.

If you are already a painter and hobbyist, you may have cultivated a great deal of this information and wish to move directly into the Instruction beyond these first pages. I certainly will not blame you for wanting to roll up your sleeves and get directly stuck into the action.

However, even if you have your first projects far behind you, perhaps you'll find something of use even in these initial basics. I'll be elaborating on the material that I use in my personal workshop and exploring the methods that I use to build, paint, and design miniature models and terrain.

So with all of that in mind, let's gather around the hearth and discuss the gear that you'll soon become the master of!

Guild Training

I know that you are likely well and ready to jump right into the action and to begin slapping paint onto miniatures with mad abandon. I would like to, if I may, initiate you into this hobby with a few basic lessons and some knowledge that will serve you well into the future as you grow and improve as a hobbyist.

With this in mind, I give you my word to be concise and to get us to the paint and brushes quickly and without too much pomp and circumstance. Some of these lessons in the Guild Training section are essential to producing outstanding results in the painting stages and—though they may lack in glamour—are part of the process and can be enjoyable too!

GUILD TRAINING I.-
PREPARATION AND THE FINE ART OF NOT HURTING YOURSELF

A brief selection of safety protocols and recommendations. This hobby is a great deal of fun, but it utilizes a wide variety of items that, if improperly used, can cause harm to the careless hobbyist.

GUILD TRAINING II.-
TOOLS OF THE TRADE

An overview of the varied assortment of brushes, paints, and hobby tools that you may wish to gather in undertaking the projects within this book. Some are essential, others are optional. Never fear, I have demarcated those groups clearly and you'll be given some directions as we move along.

Striking your way through the streets of the city, you make your way to the shabby and ill-kept tavern known as the Shattered Tankard. It leers at you in the fading light of the setting suns that paint the sky in purples and oranges. Night is coming, and that means that the clientele of this establishment is sure to become rougher.

Guild Training III. -
Thaco Thistle-Britches and The Bags of Wondrous Works

The goblin merchant Thaco Thistle-Britches is a cagey sort of merchant, and he's got the best selection of goods in the Many Realms. Each **path** in your **journey** is marked on the map in the front of this guide, and you'll need the materials listed in each of the **three bags of painting supplies and hobby tools** to work along with these lessons in each **Quest** that I will guide you through.

If you are holding this ragged tome, then it is fair to assume that you're seeking a way to express yourself through the craft of miniature painting. You seek to invoke a world of magic and myth within the manageable sizing of heroic 28-mm figures, display busts, or other figures.

You've made a fine choice in pastimes, to be sure.

This hobby is deeply rewarding, relaxing, and creative. And if you've been eyeing the task of miniature painting and still feel that it may be too daunting and difficult, then allow me to help lift the veil on that notion and put your mind at ease.

You can do this.

You may find that you are easily able to pick up these techniques and outgrow the initial lessons quickly, or you may need to repeat certain segments and take your time to review each Quest carefully before you feel confident moving forward. There is nothing wrong with either outcome.

This is not a race. It is a journey, and yours is unique and personal.

There are far too many gates and barriers that have been set before those who have considered the hobby of tabletop crafting and art, and while plenty of wonderful instruction exists both in print and on other media, much of it becomes weighed down by technical definitions and a lack of clear guidance on the subject.

Whether you are a solitary player seeking to create a tangible representation of your favorite dungeon-delving hero or a game master with the itch to build an entire campaign filled with cunning puzzles and a deadly gauntlet that spreads out in front of your players in perfect miniature detail, I believe that I can offer you some valuable assistance, but we must begin at the beginning before such glory can be celebrated.

I've been doing this for as many years as I can remember, and I have made many—if not all—of the mistakes that a beginning hobbyist, role player, and gamer could make. There is no reason that you shouldn't benefit from the hard lessons that I've learned over the decades. I believe that you can do this and produce work worthy of your pride and admiration.

As I've said, this book is your map, I am your faithful and stalwart guide, and the path before you will be defined by your choices more than mine. When you choose a gate, you will have choices to make as to how you proceed. In this book, things such as a "Tables of Contents" and numerical chapter markers are formalities and suggestions, at best. In fact, all forms of organizational arrangement are merely a latticework on which your interest and goals are led forward. Use them as you see fit.

Simply put, if you are an experienced hobbyist and wish to skip entire sections to focus on some of the more advanced techniques, may I recommend a leisurely perusal of the more basic techniques and then a deep descent into the **Journey of the Ancient Wizard**, my most advanced offering in this journal? If you're new to the entire phenomenon of tabletop storycraft and have the desire but no direction, feel free to explore the **Path of the New Apprentice**, a fulsome introduction that starts you at the very basics, and then pick and choose from the advanced offerings as you feel more confident and prepared. And don't worry—I'll be close at hand, offering what advice I have and guiding you in how you might proceed before moving on to the next Quest.

Be brave, prepare yourself for an adventure, and remember that you are the hero of this tale. Every step that we take together brings you closer to painting more confidently, with the skills necessary to produce amazing work for both display and game play.

We should head out before it gets dark. There are strange things that lurk in the woods after the three suns set . . . and you still need to gather your provisions.

There are countless knight models from a wide range of providers available at your friendly local gaming store, online retailer, or even nearby dollar store. If you want to amass a pile of plastic models to practice your painting techniques on, you need not spend your hard-earned coin on the more expensive hobby models to do it.

While you will certainly not have the level of detail and an appropriate scale for any tournament gaming, no one has written into the Code of Law that a painter must practice their skills only on models that cost them an arm and a leg. Go find yourself a bag of cheap plastic knight toys at a local store in the toy section. Lacking local options, they are available online too.

WORDS OF WARNING

Guild Training I.
PREPARATION AND THE FINE ART OF NOT HURTING YOURSELF

The tools listed here include an assortment of knives, drills, sanding boards, glues, and epoxy putties. Any of which should be used with a certain amount of caution and with the proper amount of respect for both your surroundings and your health. While I can't promise that this will be the only time that you'll witness me calling out the potential dangers of our chosen hobby, I will promise to give you a clear set of guidelines that will help you to prevent any unfortunate accidents or avoidable messes.

✠ When using glues, solvents, epoxies, accelerants, and other potentially toxic substances, do so in a well-ventilated space with the proper protection on both your work surface and your hands and face.

✠ The main glues that we will utilize are of the family of cyanoacrylate adhesives—in simpler terms—super glues. It is fully possible that in spilling a super glue on your skin that it will bond instantly, and it can even cause permanent damage to your eyes if, by some wild misuse, it ends up there. So please, take the appropriate precautions when utilizing it.

✠ A hobby knife with blades.

✠ Plastic glues are also on the menu and, while safer in some ways, are more dangerous in others, as they tend to possess stronger and more toxic fumes. So you may not glue your fingers together but the vapors that are produced should be avoided and treated with respect. A strong fan and an open window can go a long way to making your hobby preparations safe and more comfortable.

✠ Always read the labels on any hobby product and follow the safety recommendations on each individual package. Don't assume that the safety requirements for one type of glue is the same for another, even if

it's the same brand. Super glues and other chemical products can vary widely and cause you any number of figurative headaches if misused. Though, you'll likely have an actual headache as a symptom of exposure if you disregard these warnings.

✠ Knives should always be handled with care, and if you are utilizing them, make every attempt to follow the best—common sense—operating practices. Cut away from yourself, use sharp blades, and don't overuse dulled blades to produce your results. Use a mat or board to support and protect your work surface. Be certain that your model is secure and stable when scraping and cutting, and maintain a stable grip while working slowly and deliberately.

✠ When sanding or creating any amount of debris or dust through working to smooth and refine the surface of a model, wear a dust mask or respirator. Protect your eyes and wear goggles or glasses when necessary.

✠ A useful addition to the inclusion of super glue in your hobby routine is accelerator. Sometimes called "kicker," this material has a bucket of warnings attached to it and is—once again—only to be used in a well-ventilated space that is free of children and animals. It often comes in a small spray container, but I beg of you, please buy an additional dropper bottle with a fine needle applicator and minimize your exposure and the airborne nature of the spray bottle dispersion by utilizing a direct and controlled applicator.

✠ The added benefit here is that your lovely paint work will never be compromised should you need to utilize it for a repair, and the often-problematic residue will be focused only on the parts that you are attempting to bond together.

✠ Simply put, always use solvents and glues in well-ventilated areas of your home or workspace. Inhaling such chemicals can be very harmful.

Guild Training II.
TOOLS OF THE TRADE

Any discussion of hobby miniature work can easily overlook some of the simple but essential aspects of the process: a table, a chair, and proper lighting. We'll go into greater detail once we start to move through your Quests, but know that your comfort is important to the outcome of your work and the amount of time that this hobby demands makes it a key consideration.

There are a variety of items that will make your work much easier. Some are quite commonplace and easy to acquire. Let's review them together.

✦ Pipette droppers can be a very helpful addition to your arsenal of tools and will allow you to easily transfer water for mixing your paints.

✦ A cotton cloth is essential to your wipe brushes after cleaning them between colors and at the end of a paint session, as paper towels tend to fray and shed fragments that can work their way into your paint and varnishes. Paper towels have their uses but only for cleaning spills or especially messy work.

BRUSHES

One of the most common questions that I receive is "What brush should I use?" New painters want to know what size, brand, and style they should choose, and it is fully understandable. Brushes seem to be the most important tool in the arsenal of any hobby artist, and their form and function would seem to be the difference between a good result and a bad one.

I will give you the basics and an overview here, but I suggest that if you want to fully explore all the various parts of a brush, in detail, and learn about how to fully clean, store, and condition your brushes, you should skip ahead to section **B1**.

✦ A common mistake that many hobby painters make is to fill their brushes with paint and to get that paint crammed into the ferrule of the brush. The ferrule connects the bristles and the handle, and when paint dries

inside of it, not only does it become difficult to clean, but also it can—and most likely will—start to splay the bristle of your brush and ruin any hope that you may have of maintaining a useful, sharp tip.

✦ Once ruined, brushes are harder to control and get good results from. Using a poorly treated brush is much like attempting to draw a picture with a dull pencil; the results are harder to control, and greater detail becomes nearly impossible to achieve. To prevent all of this, never overfill your brush and keep the paint to—roughly speaking—the tip of the bristles to the middle of the body of the brush, called the belly.

You can review some of the diagrams included here to get a better understanding of how all of this plays out, but at the end of the day know that your goal is to carry as much material (paint) as possible and to be efficient in your painting without overloading and ruining your tools.

Caring for your equipment by cleaning your brushes with a good artist's soap will extend the working life of your brushes, whether synthetic or natural hair. Be sure to wash your brushes after each session and use a brush shaper to help maintain a sharp point.

PAINTS

When it comes to purchasing and choosing the paint that you will use in your hobby work, I have found that there are a few very serviceable, affordable, and steadfast brands available.

When choosing paint, it is important to find specially formulated brands that contain a finely ground pigment and an appropriate binder and medium. Many inexpensive craft paints are simply not up to the task and will obscure detail, refuse to bond to the model, and leave dull, uneven sheens. The easiest way to ensure that you are using material that will adhere properly to your models is to start your hobby journey with popular brands that are well respected and widely used before experimenting with acrylic paints that are perhaps not directly mixed for this application.

Avoid any cheap craft store paints, enamels, or oil paints—for now, as there are applications for all three of those forms of paint in the later stages of our explorations together. For now, stick with a basic hobby acrylic formulated for modeling, such as paints from Vallejo or Reaper Miniatures.

Acrylic paint, of any sort, type, or brand, separates when it sits on a shelf waiting to be purchased. This is because paint is made of three major components: pigment, binder, and medium. (Solvent comes into play, but I'm not going to drag it into the mix here, so we'll consider it part of the medium for the sake of simplicity.) Pigments provide the color and saturation of hue, the medium provides the method of transfer, and binder provides the adhesion for that pigment.

Paint, unlike stain, doesn't infuse itself into the subject; it sits on the surface and covers to various degrees. So the property of a paint can create different effects based on the amount of either medium or pigment that a specific product may possess.

You can find a full listing and my personal recommendations for a number of the most popular brands of hobby miniature paints in section **P1** at the end of this book. I have a full breakdown of the general qualities and widely accepted pros and cons of those various brands.

That said, we want to get you started quickly and easily in the hobby. If you are a new or inexperienced painter, you can't do better—in my humble opinion—than the basic starter sets from both Reaper Miniatures and Vallejo.

In regard to color selection, be certain that you have a number of flat sheen paints, including a basic black, white, red, blue, yellow, silver, and gold, and then add secondary colors such as purple, green, and orange as you like. Browns are helpful. Something darker and something lighter will save you a great deal of time. Magenta, cyan, and yellow could be the core that you use to replace your RGB primaries if you want to really push the flexibility and accuracy of your color mixing. To start your journey without too much complex color mixing, get the primary colors, secondary colors, and most basic metallics.

Glue

Plastic can be bonded quite nicely with a variety of easily obtained plastic glues, but I would be careful. The viscous and inexpensive tubes of hobby cement that are commonly found in art and craft stores are often more destructive and difficult to use than the inexpensive price is worth. Plastic glues operate by melting a thin layer of the plastic on both parts of your model and, once cured, fuse the pieces together in a very permanent way. The thicker and more difficult to use the glue is, the higher the likelihood is that you will be facing problems as you work.

In my experience, the inexpensive plastic cement that you might use on a model tank or plane shouldn't be used on anything at the scale of the models that we will be exploring in the tabletop gaming world. Spend a little more upfront and set yourself up for success. Seek out brands that are noted as thin or liquid poly cement.

Cyanoacrylate superglue—which possesses a great amount of utility in many applications and materials—is very commonly used across the hobby, and it is capable adhering to a wide variety of materials, including both resin and metal.

An accelerate is very helpful in the use of superglues, but be certain to read all the instructions and safety instructions.

KNIVES

Xacto blade knives are fairly easy to come across in most big box retail stores and are essential tools if you want to properly clean and prepare a variety of models, from metal to resin to plastic.

These extremely sharp blades are very useful. Don't fall into the trap of purchasing branded blades, however. I have never found that the ridiculous markup when a blade is branded to help in any tangible way in preparing a model makes it any better than a knife that was purchased at a dollar store. Save your money where you can; this hobby can be expensive and there is little sense in expending the coin on something that you can find in abundance at far lower prices than you will be given by some of the hobby professional brands.

SANDING TOOLS

The style of sanding tool that you use can be of a number of available varieties. As for the previously mentioned nail files, be aware of the wide variance of grit and flexibility. Jewelers files, needle files, and other specialty modeling file sticks are available at most craft and art outlets and stores.

Whenever working on removing material from a model, whether plastic, resin, or metal, it is a good idea to do so in a manner that prevents you from inhaling the dust and debris that can be generated when sanding is involved.

If you feel that you can't work in a well-ventilated space with ample airflow, you should purchase a dust mask that is capable of protecting you effectively. N95 is the minimum in an environment with airborne particulates and dangerous dust such as resin or metal.

WATER

When preparing your workstation, before painting, water is a key ingredient to successful hobby painting. You clean your brushes in it, dilute your points with it, hydrate your wet palette—should you rely on one—and generally utilize it to support your work from the first brush stroke to the last.

Keep your water supply, whether in a cup or old jar, as clean as possible and don't be afraid to change it out as often as you feel necessary.

Sculpting Materials

"Green Stuff" is legendary within the hobby community. It's the sculpting material that seems to rise above most others, and you can spot it used across any number of projects throughout the years. Its tale is a long and complex one, but the birthplace of this powerful substance is not the hobby desk but the kitchen sink. That is to say that it was initially created to give plumbers a substance that could be used to create powerful and permanent seals for pipes. It goes by other names and is repackaged and distributed by many hobby sources. Still, you can find more generous and cost-effective portions of this material if you search it out from venues outside of our hobby.

Milliput is a two-part sculpting product that dries to a rock-hard finish that is able to be scraped, sanded, or polished as needed. Even better, it smooths with just water and can be used to create perfectly seamless transitions between parts. It is widely available and is produced in a selection of consistencies. Superfine is the type that I use in most instances.

Both of these sculpting tools are two of the standards that are used within the hobby world to help fill gaps, convert, kit-bash, and sculpt. To correctly utilize both, you'll need a little guidance and a little bravery, but the effort can produce some amazing results and give you the ability to achieve new heights of crafting glory!

Guild Training III. -
Thaco Thistle-Britches and The Bags of Wondrous Works

The goblin Thaco Thistle-Britches shows you into his cramped and cluttered wagon; water-skins and dried rations hang from the ceiling and bundles of torches and piles of old boots sit in a corner. He is a strange creature, one with sharp features and keen, small dark eyes. As you enter into his shop, the goblin sets aside a small jar with a dozen fireflies inside of it and sizes you up suspiciously. . . .

"Oh? Another one? So soon . . . humph. What are looking at?"

You act like you haven't seen a goblin before. Yeah, I'm a goblin and—no—I'm not some bloodthirsty ne'er-do-well that seeks to ambush you in a dark cavern and steal your gold. . . . It's much more profitable to sell goods and services to those who seek a life of adventure and excitement.

My name is Thaco Thistle-Britches, proprietor of Hoof & Haversack, the fine merchant wagon that you see before you. Please, don't pet the mule; she bites.

Yes, you've got that look in your eyes. I suppose that you bought a map off of an old stranger in a tavern and now you're hell-bent on taming the great unknown?

In that case, I won't belabor the point then; you've got dragons to face and I've got inventory to sell. As stated, I sell supplies to heroic types such as yourself. Allow me to show you some of the more usual items that I just so happen in my possession at the moment.

Of course, the tools that you see here are as good as the task that you put them to, so choose a pack that fits your needs. . . ."

Thaco Thistle-Britches takes your coin, and you are free to choose one toolkit to take on your journey with you.

If you are following the map and intend to make your way to the **Kobold Caverns** following the **Path of the New Apprentice,** turn to section **B1** and open the **Raven Rucksack** to take stock of the supplies that you'll be using on your journey.

If you have already revealed the mysteries of the caverns—or are full of spit and vinegar and wish to test your skills in a more advanced adventure—you'll want to gather more effective gear and to prepare for the **Path of the Seasoned Sorcerer.** Make your way to section **B2,** open the **Eagle Knapsack,** and behold the tools of an adventurer with more than a few dents in their armor. . . .

That last pack? You better be sure that you're ready to use it before putting your hard-earned coin down on that one. It's pretty complicated adventuring gear. That said, if you're making your way to the **Wizard's Keep,** it's yours for the taking. Gather your courage and make your way to section **B3** and open up the **Owl Haversack** before making your way forward.

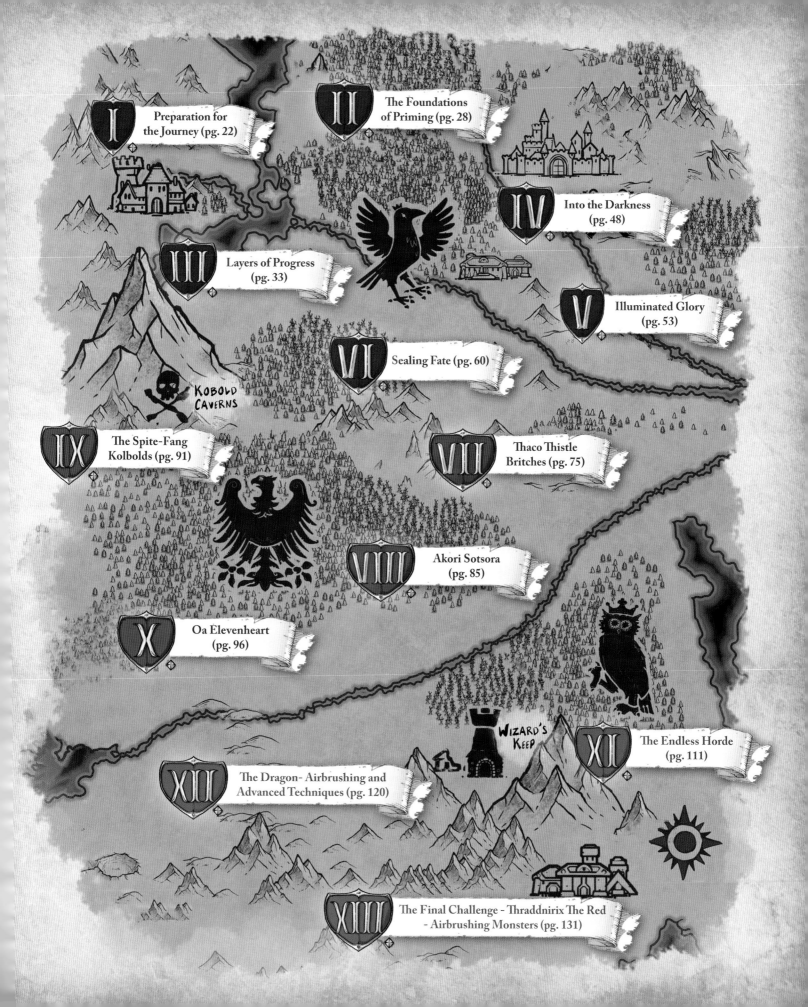

KOBOLD CAVERNS

WIZARD'S KEEP

The Path of the New Apprentice

As we undertake the first steps of our journey together, let us begin with the foundational skills and techniques that will serve you in all of the projects that you will undertake here in the collected quests within this guidebook, and beyond. With these lessons securely understood and implemented, each and every undertaking that you embark upon in the world of hobby painting and crafting will be improved!

QUEST I

PREPARATION FOR THE JOURNEY

The work that must be undertaken to clean and assemble a model before painting can begin.

QUEST II

THE FOUNDATIONS OF PRIMING

The undercoat of material that will ensure adhesion and clarity of the final layers of paint that you will later apply.

QUEST III

LAYERS OF PROGRESS

Base-coating is the first stage of painting that will provide the tone, hue, and character that will express our final work.

QUEST IV

THE SHADOWS WE CAST

A use of washing and careful shading will provide rich contrast and deep rich areas of darkness to our work in this specific process.

QUEST V

ILLUMINATED GLORY

Using successive layers of paint, we will create the illusion of light striking the highest points on the model.

QUEST VI

SEALING FATE

To protect and seal the work that we've undertaken in this process, a coat of varnish will be applied.

The Raven Rucksack - B1

This nimble set of tools is lightweight and simple.

The old leather is well worn and has seen a great deal of the world, carried on the back of a hundred adventurers.

It, clearly, has a lot of history and many tales to tell. . . .

✢ **Surface primer**—black

✢ **Acrylic hobby paints**

- 3 or 4 basic colors

- 1 or 2 metallic paints

- (See the suggested painting resources in section **R1.**)

✢ **Size 1 or 2 brush**

- (The brush should have a sharp point and be bigger than you might think. See the suggested brush resources in section **R2.**)

✢ **Hobby knife** with a few extra blades

✢ **Nail File** with a fine grit

✢ **2 cups, jars,** or **containers** for water

✢ **Palette, paper plate,** or **tile**

✢ **Paper towel, napkins,** or **cotton rag**

- (not toilet paper or tissue)

✢ Some **poster tack**

✢ **Empty spool, medicine bottle,** or bit of **wood**

✢ **Matte varnish**

The Tale of the Knights of the Myth Vale

Those that sheathe themselves in steel,
Often would pay a heavy cost
To the King they would in duty kneel,
Their lives, in war, so soon lost.

The Kobold Caverns lie beneath the Shattered Tankard Tavern. To enter the dungeon, you'll need to make your way into the wine cellar and through the secret passage down into the dank and ancient tunnels that lie within.

The map of your journey begins with a tavern and the cellar beneath. Throughout the tavern are the suits of armor that the Knights of the Myth Vale once wore in their quests to defend the realms against the tyranny of the Dragon Army. Each of the knights was issued a masterwork set of armor, and though identical in construct to those of their siblings in arms, each knight chose their own colors, sigils, and heraldry.

A Prelude to Your First Quest

Some Friendly Advice before You Begin

The Knights of the Myth Vale are little more than dusty relics and the legends of bards, but their armor is going to be the focus of a great many of our lessons in this portion of the book.

✠ You can use a single model over and over for the majority of these exercises, stripping the paint off and continuing onward. Or you can line up multiple knights as you complete them until you have made an impressive stretch of suits of armor that you can field in a tabletop game of your choosing. Or they can simply adorn a shelf or trophy case!

✠ Regardless, nothing that we do is permanent. Don't be concerned about making mistakes or being perfect at any of the techniques that we examine. These skills require practice and patience to master.

✠ If you would like to seek out a copy or more of this exact model, you can order it directly from heroforge.com. They are offering any adventurer from these lands the ability to collect the digital STL (3D) files or a physical copy at a healthy discount and have two free options for you to download.

Before we investigate some of the more advanced techniques in this tome, we must first take a sharp look at the basics of miniature painting and hobby modeling. If you are the sort of meticulous and careful adventurer who studies the entirety of a situation before moving onward, then—as you can see from the map at the front of this guidebook—this is your first step into the world of painting and our first keystone.

While the custom 3D model knights that I will be using in this first path are built with a particular eye toward the forms, shapes, and textures that best illuminate the techniques that we will be addressing, you may find any model of the general style of this knight and use that in your personal exercises.

We are seeking a model with open, simple shapes: no flesh—for now—and a combination of fabric and metal shapes.

You may want some assistance in making the color combination choices that will be used on your Knight of the Myth Vale. Never fear—I will walk you through the process of color selection and usage in a later section. But meanwhile, let's start our work with the story that we wish to impart upon the simple knight we will be using as our first painting tutorial.

Who is this figure? Where do they come from? What is their story?

How does their past reflect upon their appearance?

If this sort of mental acrobatics seems intimidating, don't be concerned. I have provided you with a series of enjoyable charts that you can utilize to make these decisions easier. Maybe you'll see something that inspires you and you'll want to expand upon it. That's perfectly fine. Or perhaps you wish to ignore the charts entirely and tell your own tales!

Please don't let me or a handful of charts stand in your way! As with so many of the tools that I hope to impart to you, your experience and needs will define how and what you use here.

So find your own pace and rhythm, use what you want, and ignore the rest!

The Hand of Fate - A Knight to Remember

Roll 3 D6 (six-sided dice) to determine the story of your
Knight of the Myth Vale:

3-7	This knight was born to a simple farming village and always kept true to their humble beginnings, seeking simple colors and reminders of the earth beneath their feet. They prefer neutral tones and avoid anything garish or bright.
8-10	Here is the great defender known as the Shield of Faith! They lived their life as a cleric of the Arcanan god of justice and hope, Solvir Tor, before laying down their vestment and picking up a sword and shield. They abhor violence but will always protect those in need. They cherish the pure and clean tones and hues of their former faith. Light, airy colors represent their holy connection.
11-12	Aha! You found the Jester of Mirth Hill, a knight with a very free and rambunctious approach to life. Bright colors and deep, saturated tones are the favorites of this warrior. They love wine and song, so find colors that speak to you of frivolity and jovial living.
13	An ill omen . . . you have discovered a hidden armor that was meant to be forgotten. The Traitor Knight wore this cursed and charred armor. It is infused with dark and forbidden magics and is cloaked in the shadow and hues of evil and vile coloration. Fear this armor and remember the lessons that were taught in this knight's failing.
14-18	Before you stands the armor of the Knight of Seaward Point. They stood vigil for three years on the isle of Ruuwar and sailed with the great Captain Navi Illawye. They bore the colors of the sea upon their cloak and shield, and their finely polished armor carried the colors of the great oceans within the sheen of the steel.

The **Hand of Fate** system is going to be present for you to use throughout all of your adventures in the Many Realms!

You'll need a full set of polyhedral dice for many of the exercises in this guidebook, but if you don't own any (and have access to the Inter-Web), simply summon any of the free dice apps that are easily available through a great many sources. **(Check the resources listed in section R3.)** Use your dice rolls to help you create narrative choices, formulate challenges for yourself, and keep your hobby exercises fresh and unique.

Just look for the **Hand of Fate** symbol on the maps and in various sidebars throughout your quest.

Quest I

PREPARATION FOR THE JOURNEY

CLEANING MODELS

Hobby models and miniatures come in a wide variety of styles and types. If you're reading these words, I doubt that you're a stranger to the seemingly endless parade of plastic, resin, and metal miniatures that can be found in neat rows at your friendly local gaming store and online. Quite frankly, it can be simultaneously exhilarating and daunting to make a selection worthy of your time and effort.

Each miniature that you decide to paint is going to represent a certain amount of your personal and free time. Aside from the price of the piece itself, which can be considerable; after all, you are investing your labor into the final product as well.

Once you've made the decision as to which miniature is going to become the focus of your artistic ambitions, put down your hard-earned coin, made the journey back to your home, and sat yourself down at a table with your spoils, the real journey—and hard work—begins.

✛ Every model, no matter where it has come from, will require some amount of preparation before you even pick up a paintbrush. To do that, you'll need to assess the requirements of the specific model that you've chosen. If it's a boxed set or a more complex sculpt, it may include some instructions that offer wildly varying degrees of guidance.

✛ It is more likely, when dealing with simpler single miniatures, that you'll be left to your own devices in interpreting the clues that have been left to you in assembling your model. This could be as simple as gluing an arm in place or attaching the figure to a base.

✛ If you're following the Quest, the simple knight model that you see in the example is a single piece, but that doesn't mean that it doesn't require some work to bring it up to the level that will produce the best possible results when everything is primed, painted, and finished.

✛ Once you've ensured that you are properly protecting yourself and those around you, assess the model that you will be working on and consider your options in preparing and constructing your model.

✛ The basics are simple, and as recommended in your **B1 Pack**, you'll be using superglue, a nail file, and a hobby knife with replaceable blades to clean and prepare this model.

SCRAPE

I prefer to work my way from the interior of a model to the exterior details one tool at a time, starting with the most destructive process and working toward the most refined of the preparation processes.

For instance, on the knight model in our Quest:

✛ Begin with a hobby knife and remove any imperfections and blemishes that may be left from sprue, molds, or supports from a 3D printer.

✛ Seek out the thin lines that may rest on the smooth surfaces of the model. If you follow the sides of the model, you should be able to determine whether there are any mold lines that need to be scraped gently away with your hobby blade.

✛ If your model was created with a 3D printer, it may have small dots that represent the last of the supports that held the model aloft during the printing process. They can be easily handled by sliding the edge of your blade along the surface of your model away from you.

✛ If the model—or parts of it—was removed from a sprue, be certain the points that connected the model to the sprue are as flat and smooth as possible. Don't leave unnecessary nubs behind; your bladework can make their appearance a distant memory.

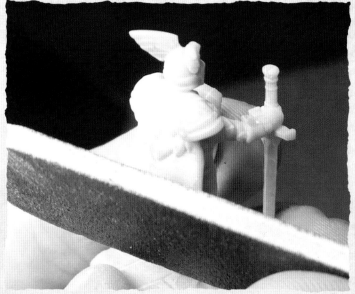

Sand

✢ Once the mold lines or connection points are cleared away, gently smooth the areas with a fine-grit nail file, working in short back-and-forth or small, circular motions, stopping as often as needed to check the part and ensure that you are not removing too much material.

✢ The goal here is to produce a surface that is smooth and free of any foreign debris that is not part of the original sculpt.

✢ The right tool is, as always, a question that you will ultimately need to answer on your own based on the material that you are working with and the amount of flash and molding line that you wish to remove. A coarse grit is going to quickly remove larger amounts of plastic, resin, or pewter, but you are sacrificing a great deal of control for the advantage of strength and speed. That said, using too fine of a grit when working to knock down some difficult mold lines and sprue scars may leave you frustrated, as your work will take much longer to complete. Keeping a selection of grits is helpful; step down to a finer grit as you polish and perfect the work.

✢ If you only have access to a hobby blade, it is fully possible to produce a smooth surface without the files at all. Depending on the model that you are working on, the use of any of these tools is dependent fully on your needs and the standard that you are seeking to achieve.

WASH

You may discover that the miniature you're working with is coated in a thin layer of mold release that aids in the removal of the cured resin material from the molds used to cast the figure in. This is also, from time to time, an issue with both plastic and metal miniatures.

✦ If you want to prevent any issues with paint and primer adhesion, it is a good operating procedure to wash your miniature in warm, soapy water and gently scrub it with a cheap toothbrush.

✦ Be certain to rinse the figure off and to allow it to fully dry before moving forward to any future steps within this process.

✦ Is this essential? To be honest, more often than not I've rolled the dice and moved to priming immediately, but it is a risk. My rule of thumb is just that. Using my thumb, if I feel any greasiness or slickness on the model that I am working on, I take the time to undergo the wash stage.

✦ If I move forward without a pre-priming wash and my primer isn't adhering, or if I see any strange sheens or uneven finishes once the primer is dry, I will—cursing myself and my rashness—strip the miniature and begin anew after a fresh start, including the bubble bath.

✦ Resin and metal models are particular in their production and require washing more often than plastic.

✦ In section **R1** I include some instructions for using some simple and safe household cleansing products to strip off paint and primer so that you can start over.

GLUE

Depending on the model that you are working on, different glues may be used. Determine what works best for you based on the material that you are working with. Below, you'll find the first of my explanations and suggestions on the subject.

✦ If you are using a cyanoacrylate superglue—which possesses a great amount of utility in many applications and materials—do so with a sparing application. "Less is more" has never been truer than in the application of superglue. It is possible to use so much glue that you make the bonding process between parts weaker. The goal should always be to use the least amount of glue possible while still achieving a secure bond.

✦ A thin bead on a single side of the model should serve you in most situations. A rough surface will always bond more easily than a smooth one, so—if it is needed—run your hobby blade across the surfaces to "score" them on the bonding sides before applying the adhesive and pressing them together. Also, be certain that the surface is clear of any dust or debris, as it can weaken the bond if loose material mixes into the glue.

✦ Regardless of the glue that you use, always maintain the tips of the bottles and edges of any lids by carefully wiping them down after use to prevent clogging, drying, and bonding of the lids or caps. Taking care to clean and store your glues properly will ensure that you are able to rely on them when they are next called into service.

When building a model, I like to clean and prepare all the parts and then place them on a cutting mat or cardboard surface to protect the table underneath. We'll use this same surface throughout our time together, so set it up in an easily accessible place that allows you to remain seated comfortably for hours at a time.

After doing a number of "dry fits" on the model, I will score any parts that I feel require a little more roughness to their surfaces to allow for a strong and healthy bond. Should two parts present a particular issue, due to the weight and position of those pieces, I'll cut a small bit of wire and drill two holes to "pin" the model together. This technique is advanced and thankfully oftentimes unnecessary.

The bloodstains on the floorboards when you enter confirm your suspicions, and you keep the sword at your hip close at hand as you step to the barkeep and order a drink. With a well-placed tip of a silver coin, she allows you to enter the cellar, and you make your way into the darkened corridors that will lead you on your first adventure. It's dark and dank, and rats are running through the shadows around you as prepare yourself for the unknown. . . .

Most modern models are lightweight plastic and expertly divided so that when reassembled, they are offered the support that they require, thanks to the forethought that was put in by the sculptors and manufacturers.

In our final chapters, you will find a simple guide to pinning your models . . . you can find a simple guide to pinning your models and some discussion on why and when it may be a good idea, as well as a brief overview later in this section. Head to the **Hero's Rest** at the back of the guidebook if you are keen to get a jump on such secrets. (We'll wait for you here.)

Once the model is fully assembled, glued, and free of any flash and mold lines, while it might be tempting to move directly into the priming sections of your journey, take a moment to assess your subject. If you find that there are spaces present between the joining pieces, you should decide whether you want to spend the time to fill the gaps and perfect the surfaces that make up your miniature.

Certainly, you may, at this point, leave the model alone and allow it to serve whatever purpose that you have set for it. In preparing and building an entire army of skeletons, space aliens, or goblins, you may not wish to expend the extra effort to manage the minor imperfections that typically arise at this stage. Like so much of our work here, the end result is up to the time that you have to invest in refining the projects that you are working on with such steps.

Gap Filling

Gap filling can be done with a number of products, but I'll keep things focused and simple by mentioning the hobby standards and most popular items to use.

For most uses, you'll find that **Milliput** and **Green Stuff** will serve our purposes well.

With both of these products, you'll discover that they are separated into two parts. To create a workable putty, you'll need to segment off equal parts of each portion and mix them together. With Milliput, you'll just need to keep your fingers wet to prevent the material from sticking to your fingers; with Green Stuff, I recommend that you keep a little aloe vera gel close at hand.

Knead the material until it is fully blended and begin to separate it into small beads and ropes that will serve to fill the gaps that you may be facing on your model. Using your fingers, while wearing protective gloves or using metal sculpting tools or silicone color shaper brushes, you can insert the putty and smooth it into place, eliminating any spaces or gaps that may be standing between you and miniature perfection.

If necessary, assuming that you haven't quite smoothed the material perfectly, you can sand the dried material gently using the same tools that we used to prepare the model earlier on.

Pinning

Pinning a model can be the best way to ensure that the figure survives the day-to-day—and night-to-night—handling while you use it in the war game or role-playing adventure of your choice.

You can learn about the various types of pin vices that are available and how to use them elsewhere in this book, but for now, the basics are explained here.

A metal rod (a bit of steel paper clip or brass rod, usually) is adhered within two drilled holes in the connecting parts of the figure, creating a much stronger and sturdier bond that is certain to last.

Often an accelerator can be used to help expedite the drying of glue, but it should be used with extreme caution, as it is toxic and should not find its way on your skin or, worse, in your eyes or mouth. If you're a younger hobbyist, this is one of the items in our arsenal that requires parental support!

There is a chemical reaction that occurs immediately once superglue (cyanoacrylate) and an accelerator come in contact with one another. That reaction leaves you very little room for adjustment, so be certain to dry fit the parts of the model together before applying glue and accelerator.

Sculpting

Sculpting is a skill that requires as much practice and attention as painting and is intricately tied to the roots and development of the miniature hobby. Originally, models for tabletop role-playing games and war games were sculpted by hand and cast in lead and pewter. Some companies still hold true to the same techniques and manufacturing methods that were used widely at the birth of the craft, but most have evolved to the much more precise use of 3D sculpting software and overseas manufacturing, which requires the creation of a metal die from which the plastic models are injection molded.

Resin manufacturing is much simpler and more common in smaller, more boutique operations. These models are cast much in the same way as the older pewter figures were created and, as such, can give the creators more freedom to make varied runs based on demands.

Handling the Model

The last topic that we should cover before we move forward in your journey is how to best manage the model that you'll be painting. Up until now, we've been assembling and cleaning and preparing your subject—a series of fairly indelicate processes in the way of worrying much about the surfaces of the model as you work.

From this point forward, however, you'll be applying paint and coats of wet color in the form of ink and wash, base coats, and highlights. Any of these layers and the hard work that you will put into them can be undone by a misplaced thumb or wayward finger, smudging and smearing your careful blends and artful progress left in ruin.

To prevent this, there are some simple and inexpensive solutions that can be implemented to protect your work and help you to control and maneuver your grip and allow access to the model in a much more adaptive and careful way.

✠ A wood block, spool, empty medicine bottle, or other object of your choosing can be repurposed to allow you to attach your model securely by the base with a little poster tack, superglue, or double-sided tape.

✠ Once mounted, you'll find that you are easily able to progress through the future stages of this journey without risking a minor catastrophe or unfortunate smearing or smudging.

Congratulations!

You've navigated your very first Quest within this guide and are well on your way to the main attraction: actually putting paint on the miniature that you've prepared. As every intrepid painter before you has learned, the time that you spend now will elevate your work and set you up for success throughout your journey as a hobby artist!

With your newfound knowledge and a little bit of practice, you'll soon discover that you are able to deftly maneuver a wide variety of situations that often occur in assembling and cleaning up a model before painting it. Truthfully, there is a wealth of time-saving techniques that will aid you in these stages as you improve and grow.

We'll discuss shortcuts and speed work in the **Path of the Ancient Wizard**, or you are welcome to leap ahead if you want an overview. Just be sure to return to this milestone so that we can continue on to **Quest II**!

It's the very foundation on which every one of your paint strokes will be built and the basis for long-lasting and easy applications! We're just a few short steps away from really getting creative, so let's keep exploring!

Quest II

THE FOUNDATIONS OF PRIMING

PRIMING WITH A BRUSH

"What is primer? Why should we use it in our hobby painting?"

Those are fair questions, and I can answer them for you with a little explanation, some examples, and a touch of cautionary warning.

I think that it is safe to say that as hobby painters, when we spend hour upon hour neatly painting our models, we hope that they are able to weather the most basic handling and minor bumps and bruises that invariably occur when a figure is put into the world of battlefield game play or a life of sheltered display.

Primer gives us a more resilient product that adheres more fully to the surfaces of plastic, metal, or resin.

Simply put, a primer is a specially formulated paint that contains more powerful binding agents that provide the mixture stronger resilience and a better texture to layer other paint material on top of.

It will prevent chipping and scratching that can occur quite easily without it and will lengthen the life of the work that you put into painting your model.

TYPES OF PRIMERS

Primers come in a wide variety of colors—just like regular paint—and the choice of color that you decide to use can lend some tone to the layers of paint that you add afterward. In the hobby painting community, the three most popular choices are **black, white,** and **gray,** but others are available and have their uses.

Additionally, primers are available in a variety of applications. "Rattle-can" spray, brush-on, and airbrush are the most common, but I imagine that someone is applying primer through the use of a trebuchet somewhere in the world. Stick to the first three tones during your early works and get creative once you find your sea legs.

✦ Primer has tooth, and that texture allows for good adhesion between your primer and the model itself.

✦ For the Knight of Myth Vale, we'll be using a traditional brush technique. If you prefer, and have some experience, use the method that works best for you. . . .

Brush primer is available in many colors and can be purchased in larger containers that will last you for the majority of your hobby career. I prefer Vallejo, but many brands are available.

Spray primer (called "rattle can" by some disreputable types) is available in a variety of colors and brands. I recommend that you use a spray that is specifically created for use on models.

Airprush primer is the most complex and labor intensive of the choices presented here, but it is the most versatile and effective of the three. The finish is thin, easy to control, and complete.

In this Quest, we are going to be applying our black primer with a large brush and allowing it to dry fully. This is as simple as it sounds, but let's be clear about the process, and then I'll go into a bit of the options that open up to us when we utilize white or gray primers. In later Quests, I'll give you my full guidance on using both aerosol cans and airbrushes. For our

purposes here, the brush is perfectly appropriate and will give us the results that we need to move forward.

Be certain that the material that you are using is, in fact, a primer. Simple black or white paint will not provide you with the benefits of an actual primer.

The creak of old lumber rings out in the darkened cellar as you venture forward, fumbling in the pack that the goblin, Thaco Thistle-Britches sold you. Rope, dried rations, bandages, a brick of chalk, a small roll of red yarn. . . . The pack was full of all of the assorted tools and items that any amateur adventurer could require in exploring the depths of ancient barrows and forgotten dungeons, but where was the blasted lantern!?!

Then you find the tinder twigs and a small wax candle. You light the candle, and the warm light of the flickering flame dances across the hard-packed dirt walls of the cellar of the old, rundown tavern. Another rat charges out of the darkness and rushes pass your boot as you move forward past the rows of dusty old wine bottles and massive wooden barrels and kegs.

Arm Yourself

There are a number of essential tools that you'll require whenever you apply paint to a miniature. Namely, you'll need a brush and a palette or some form of surface to mix your paint on. If you don't have a cheap plastic palette—the sort that you can pick up at any arts and crafts store—use an old plate or a plastic lid from a kitchen container. Just be certain that it is waterproof and that it can sit level on your work surface.

*Travel forth to the special section **B1** for a fulsome exploration of the subject of caring for and using your brushes.*

For this task, we don't need to rely on a small detail brush. As you'll learn in section **B1**, there are a variety of sizes in the world of brushes. For our purposes, you'll want at least a **size 2 brush** with a nice sharp tip and well-kept bristles. If you own an expensive sable hair paintbrush, this isn't the place to start using it quite yet. I recommend a plain old nylon or synthetic brush of a decent size. Trust me—it is more than adequate in the priming stages.

Primer is a rougher, coarser material by definition, and while it functions much like traditional acrylic paint, it does, by its formulation, wear down brushes much more quickly. There is little reason to put an expensive brush to work on this task, and a decent synthetic is just fine to do the legwork required here.

With your palette—or makeshift palette—close at hand, get the very last item that you'll need to begin your work: a cup with clean water in it.

If you've bought your primer recently, it's going to require some additional care before we get started.

With our black primer prepared and ready for use on the palette, draw small amounts of paint up in the bristles at no more than 50 percent of the belly of the brush.

When applying primer, I find that it helps the final finish of the figure to paint a stripe of paint and then another, blending the two with a small bit of overlap.

I find that rolling the tip across the palette keeps the tip of the brush sharp and ready for work on the varied surfaces of the model.

Marrying edge to edge, work your way around the miniature until you have covered the entirety of it with a thin coat.

Prime Tips for Primers

Primer isn't the same as regular paint. It contains resins and other bonding agents that make it much more powerful in its ability to bond to surfaces, and it can contain additional material that—on a very fine level—creates a texture that the regular paint will be able to adhere to.

At this point, I will state that one of the most difficult—and important—things that you will ever learn in this hobby is learning how to understand the thickness of the paint that you are working with and how to alter it and change the consistency of it to provide the most effective coverage on your miniature.

It is a crucial skill, not an easy thing to master, and something that takes practice and patience.

On that subject, I will also state that while understanding consistency and application is something that we can—and will—explore thoroughly here, it is ultimately something that requires a good amount of hands-on experience to successfully implement. Just keep painting and experimenting!

Every paint, primer, glaze, and ink will behave a little differently, depending on a wild number of variables. When dealing with primers in particular, test out your material and focus on achieving a clean, clear application that doesn't obscure any detail.

There are—of course—methods and ratios that can help you to know that you are on the right track during your work. In **Quest III**, you'll find a sidebar that breaks all of this down for you in a way that I feel will help you along the way as you experiment, practice, and improve.

The Best Practices for Priming Your Models

✛ For your first prime coat, we are seeking a smooth layer of material that will cover the entire model but not obscure the detail or dry in a way that creates unwanted texture.

✛ Avoid watery pooling.

✛ The general rule of thumb is to seek a material consistency that is that of heavy cream—milky and slightly translucent.

✛ You may discover that you have—directly out of the bottle—a perfectly smooth and workable primer paint. However, most of the time, the chances are that your primer consistency isn't going to be perfect. Don't fret! This is something that we can learn to handle easily.

✛ Once you place the primer on your palette, fill your brush with some clean water out of your painting cup and place a few drops next to the primer and mix them together gently. Once you feel that you are achieving a "heavy cream" consistency, you're ready for application.

✛ A prime coat should be neat, but at the end of the day, it's going to be covered with another layer, depending on your techniques. It's best not to get too obsessed with the idea of perfection. A solid, clean coat, applied quickly, will do the trick. A second coat may be necessary.
Move on as soon as you can!

The Hand of Fate - Elemental Spirits

Roll 1 D4 (one four-sided die) to determine the story of your *Knight of the Myth Vale:*

1	The power of **earth** has guided you. You trust the rocks and stones of the world and are sturdy and reliable.
2	**Fire** is your path, and you do not conceal your rage when invoking power. You are quick to act and slow to forgive.
3	As quick and nimble as the wind, **air** is your guide and your path as broad as the sky itself. You are free in all things.
4	Ever changing, ever seeking new experiences, your hand is led by the power of the **water**, and learning and understanding are your salvation.

APPLICATION OF BRUSH-ON PRIMERS

After that, it's all about application. While we will be exploring the technique fully, our focus here is on complete, thin coats that join each other on the wet edges. Work your way across the miniature, keeping your brushstrokes from top to bottom—more or less. Each section will require some judgment, but always work to make your application smooth, avoiding pooling and clotting.

✠ If, once applied, you can still see the bare plastic, resin, or metal underneath the primer, apply a second coat. But don't do so until the first coat is completely dry. Ignoring that step will result in deeper issues, as you might start moving about the half-dried coat and create chunky blobs and streaks that will show through to every stage after this one.

✠ Let your paint dry before applying more—unless you are intentionally wet blending and layering your paints. (*More on that in our discussions of advanced techniques in later Quests.*)

✠ If necessary, review my tips regarding using a hair dryer to expedite your work and speed up your workflow. That weapon of fiery fury is fully discussed in sections later on along with some other techniques that may help you in speed painting and in expediting your finishing work.

In Conclusion . . .

Priming is essential, but once you understand the process and work to perfect this foundational step, you'll find that everything that comes after is much easier and your results are all the better for your early efforts and dedication to the foundations of your work.

In **Quests X–XII** we'll examine the use of airbrushes and how they can improve our techniques. Priming is certainly an area that is improved from the use of such technology. Even sooner, in **Quests VII–IX** we'll use rattle-can, off-the-shelf spray primers, to quickly and evenly prime our models. If you like, jump ahead to learn all about it.

If you do travel onward to those sections, move over to the material lists in the Path of Seasoned Sorcerer and the Way of the Ancient Wizard so that you are properly equipped for those adventures.

Quest III

LAYERS OF PROGRESS

BASE COATING

"How can base coating be done effectively and efficiently?"

Within this Quest, we will examine the core skill that much miniature painting instruction focuses upon, base coating. Base coating your model can be a complicated matter, but, as with so much of our work here, I encourage you to join me in a careful examination of the most key elements of the subject and then to layer on—this joke will be funny later on; trust me—the more complex elements of the subject as we progress through our work here.

To begin with, let's move as quickly, deliberately, and bravely to the point where we can put paint onto our primed and prepared model and build upon our experience as we continue to learn and improve. To better yourself in this craft, you must work at it. Over and over again, as often as possible, practice painting to hone your skills.

There are a great many suggested techniques and methods that can be employed in putting base colors onto your miniatures before moving onto advanced finishing techniques. I'll walk you along the path here and share the skills that I've found worth the effort of mastering. Perhaps more importantly, I will attempt to illuminate a wide variety of techniques that will allow you to look at your model and make clear, well-

thought-out decisions that will help you to define and explore color choice, storytelling, and style.

It is easy to become distracted by the advanced techniques that await us beyond the basic techniques that we are going to utilize here in this Quest. When you see images of washes and dry brushing, wet blending and two-brush blending, inking and nonmetallic metal, it can be frustrating to hammer away at the techniques that surround base coating a model. But without a clear understanding of the methods required to produce the foundational painting upon which all those techniques are built, we'd be putting the cart before the horse.

Stay with me and let's review the key skill set that will provide us with a springboard for the advanced methods that we will undertake in later Quests.

Before we begin, let's explore the subject of paints. I recommend that you move to sections **P1** and **B1** and wander through the listings that I have compiled there for you. Many of the initial questions that I field from burgeoning painters are centered around material selections and, specifically, my choice of paint and brushes.

It certainly is understandable. The brushes that you use and the paints that you paint with are the most important tools that you will use in your work as you spend hours upon hours painting miniatures.

What brushes to use in these lessons?

For base-coating brushes, stick to something around a 2. You want a brush with a healthy belly to carry paint and a sharp tip to allow you to control your applications.

Are You Ready?

The process is simple at the level that we are working at, but that doesn't have to mean boring or flat. Learning to focus on and skillfully use a smaller range of color is a very valuable skill.

Additionally, I know that the mountains of products available on hobby store shelves and online can be both intimidating and overwhelming. I think that it serves us well to focus on what is essential and to learn to create colors using a limited selection of paint, rather than buying two or three hundred separate premixed paints to utilize in producing results for every eventuality of color and tone.

So you need ten or so paints and three or so brushes. Your palette is still in play here, plus a few paper towels and a fresh and clean cup of water.

If you are already deep in some manner of advanced work and want to learn about the use of wet palettes, then travel to the back of the book and dig into my instructions on the proper usage and preferred methods to make use of that tool. To be clear, I don't see it as essential in this stage of our journey. It's a nice addition to your arsenal, but it doesn't make you a better painter; it just hydrates your paint and makes it easier for you to be a better painter when you are prepared for the added complication. A white ceramic tile that cost half a dollar can be very effective and, while not keeping your paint hydrated, is still viable and sometimes the right tool for the job.

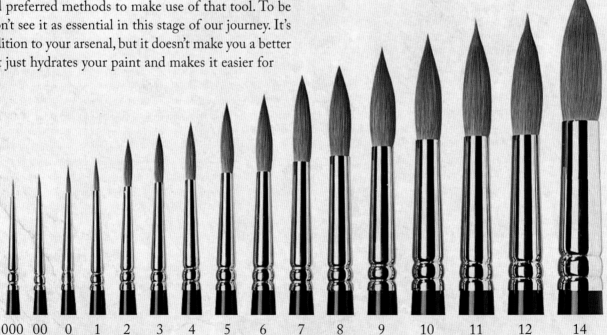

| 000 | 00 | 0 | 1 | 2 | 3 | 4 | 5 | 6 | 7 | 8 | 9 | 10 | 11 | 12 | 14 |

The black primer may show through the first base coats, as you can see here. Don't worry about it at this stage. Once dry, we'll be adding another coat and maybe a third!

The second and third coats will make the final result opaquer but will help the model retain the detail and won't clog the miniature with thick, chunky layers that dull the model.

Again, don't overfill your brush. Draw paint into the belly at roughly 50 percent of the bristles and begin slowly applying your first coats, layering one stroke after the next.

With each of our chosen colors, we work much in the same manner as the first: even, thin coats that blend on the edges with the next stroke. Allow each coat to dry fully.

Maintaining a comfortable grip on the handle and the brush is important in creating a stable target for you to use your brushwork on. Find ways to improve your comfort and control!

Leaving very small areas of black primer exposed in the deep recesses can be beneficial when working quickly to create an instantaneous panel liner effect that will contrast and create visual separation.

Did you use the first Hand of Fate tool that I placed for you at the beginning of the Knights of the Myth Vale Quest path? It's there to help you make some key decisions that often aren't discussed in miniature painting, and you'll find more of them as we continue forward from this point.

Choosing the colors that you will use on any miniature comes with a collection of questions that can cause hesitation for even the most experienced and skilled hobbyist. It's something that becomes easier as you progress in the hobby, but everyone who undergoes this craft finds themselves stuck on color choice and stylistic consideration from time to time.

It is my hope that some of the exercises and other creative challenges that are offered here will give you tools that help you in the process of color selection and that you are inspired to make bold decisions. These little helping hands will always be here for you to come back to when seeking ways to spark some creativity and help you to determine new directions for your work that you may have overlooked beforehand.

Each Hand of Fate page has a mark on the **Journey Map** in the front pages of the book, and you can also easily spot them by the hand sigils on the top corner of the page.

Use them as you like, not just for the specific Quest that they may relate to but to help create a dynamic and elaborate story that leads you to creative discovery and growth. If you are stuck on a project, walk through the Hand of Fate and see whether lightning strikes!

As we approach our first miniature, a basic knight, we'll need to determine the colors that we are going to use in defining the story that we have created either independently or through the use of the creative tools within this book. For the first knight that we'll be painting, I've chosen green, white, gold, and silver.

I'll mix a brown for the fur on the cloak and use a black wash to shade a little later on.

Simplicity is our goal here. There will be plenty of time to explore advanced techniques and more dynamic color schemes, but simple can be extremely effective, and our goal here is to build confidence through repetition and a keen understanding of the basic skills that we are using.

Whether this is your first miniature or the five-thousandth, I invite you to undertake this process with the focus on creating a clean and simple result without pressure or judgment. This model is your opportunity to improve your skills and truly home in on the most key and pure elements of the base-coating process.

Something seems strange . . .

The solitary figure standing in the dark corner of the musty cellar of the Shattered Tankard Tavern startles you. You had felt the gaze of something in the flickering light of the wax candle, but you weren't sure until this moment.

Upon closer inspection, you discover that—much like the abandoned suits of full plate mail armor that lined the walls of the common room upstairs—this lurking figure is nothing more than a forgotten relic from an age long past.

This suit of plate, more than the others, is further along in its decay. Its surface is covered in heavy rust, and it shield is broken on the stone floor. . . .

The strange old man had sold you the dried parchment map with a wry smile, before warning you that the adventures that it would lead you to might test you further than you expected and to follow only the paths that you felt prepared for.

The old man had muttered something about riddles and the impetuousness of the restless and the fate of treasure seekers. He was strange, to be certain. But now, standing in front of the old armor suit, you produce the rolled parchment and open it, revealing a labyrinth of dark black ink marks, scrawled notes, and ancient glyphs.

A Fair Shake

Acrylic paint is, as we've discussed elsewhere, created with a number of components that give it the properties that we expect from it so that it can perform the key requirements of the material. We need it to adhere to the surface of the model, and we need it to transfer an amount of hue and tone in a way that conveys the desired color.

The consistency and viscosity of the paint are important as well. You may need to thin out the paint, or you may be able to use it immediately as dispensed from the bottle. It isn't a set science, and you will need to make an accurate judgment of the material throughout the application.

✟ There are a handful of indicators that will assist you along the way.

✟ The very first step, regardless of the brand, is to shake the paint vigorously to ensure that the binder and pigment and solvent are all fully and completely incorporated.

✟ Check the bottom of the paint pot or bottle to see whether there is any irregular color pooling. This is heavier pigment that has settled at the bottom of the container and requires that you redistribute it into the paint.

✟ When you dispense a small amount, or by examining the top of an open container, is there a clear or white liquid pooling in the tip of the dropper or the exposed layer of a pot? That is the opposite of the previous instance, as the binder is floating at the top and not thoroughly mixed into the rest of the paint.

✟ A good rule of thumb is that if you are certain that you spent enough time mixing the bottle that you are about to call to service, consider shaking it for an additional minute just to be safe. It won't hurt your paint and will eventually make your arms look like those of a mighty barbarian warrior.

Agitators—such as stainless-steel bearings or glass beads—are helpful and can be added to your paint bottles to assist you in stirring the paint while you shake it. Vortex shakers and other high-tech options are luxury products, to be sure, but can be found on the desks of many serious painters. I'll list some resources in section **R2** at the end of this guidebook to help your explorations.

Different elements on any model will have different textures. For now, simply work to add a clean, clear base coat to each of the major areas. There will be plenty of time to expand on it.

Turning the model around by the handle, work to fill in the major areas of interest on the model and alter your position and grip as needed, moving the model and your brush as one.

Your real goal in this exploration should be to discover what works best for you and to leave the rest by the wayside.

As we move forward, bravely, and undertake the task of painting our miniature with the foundational colors that will form the sturdy basis of our future work, know that for every miniature painter and hobbyist you speak to, you will find differing approaches to this and most of the keystone techniques and stages in the craft.

At this stage of your journey, your goal is to practice and try a variety of methods, to pick and choose the elements that will ultimately become the skills and processes that comprise your personal hobby arsenal. While many utilize specific techniques, you'll find just as many versions and variations of those techniques. The same is true of almost every tip and trick, skill, and challenge that I am guiding you through.

It's best to just practice and try new variations as you discover them. There are a thousand ways to skin a dragon, and you won't know which way is best for you until you get your hands dirty.

Paint two or three models using the simple methods that I've outlined in this Quest and then start to mix things up.

Once you practice enough and experiment with paint consistency and brush control, you'll find that you stop thinking consciously about a great many things that intimidate new and beginning painters. Nothing that I tell you will replace experience, and you owe it to yourself to work at a pace that gives you the freedom to fail.

Now, let's move onward and make some magic. Base coating is just the beginning....

The Hand of Fate - Shield Crest

 Roll 2 D100 (two ten-sided dice) designating one die as the tens digit and one as the singles digit. Should you be lucky enough to achieve a roll of double zero, know that result is a 100. A zero in the tens is just that.

01-20	Within a grand and magnificent city, your knight is the follower of an ancient and holy order and has served the temple for many years. Your sigil is a ***great bird,*** and you bear the mark upon you.
21-40	You were lost in the distant desert lands to the south for many months, where you survived on the blood and body of the snakes that you found in that desolate place. The ***wise snake*** is your symbol to remind you of your will to survive.
41-60	As the champion of the Sovereign of the Land, you are marked by the ***mighty lion*** and fiercely protect the honor of the people and rulers of your homeland. You serve and serve well, wearing the mark of your station and the oath that you spoke to your beloved liege.
61-80	Having raised yourself up from the fishing villages from the east, you learned about the legends of the great powers of the ***clever fish*** and how kingdoms have been raised or fallen by the grace and will of the waterborne beings that brought both food and prosperity.
81-100	You have always been a wanderer. In the forests you found your way, and in those verdant places your oath was born, made to the forest spirits and the fae that showed themselves to you once your heart was shown to be aligned with their whims. The ***fleet stag*** is your totem.

Determine the totem that best represents your knight and use the results to make decisions in your themes and color choices.

While you may use the symbol literally on the shield, try to find ways to express the relation to the motif of your figure without purely literal representation.

Feel free to wildly and creatively elaborate on what—specifically—the symbol is.

(Example: **Great bird** could be a falcon or a vulture. The choice is yours.)

Whether you are using a wet palette, a traditional cup palette, or a paper plate, I find that it is always a good bit of preparation to select the colors and schemes before you begin painting. This means that you will need to decide on a set of colors to paint with, and that requires some hard choices—choices that can cause any painter, old or new, to stall in a mire of indecision before even picking up a brush.

This is all to say that if you are stuck, take a moment and retreat to the map at the very front of this guidebook. Seek out the Hand of Fate markers and begin moving through the prompts that they provide. Some are more specific and direct than others, but all of them are meant to initiate your creative spirit and give you the confidence to move forward with any project that you are undertaking.

It never hurts to ask yourself about the story behind the figure that you've chosen to paint. What is their life like? Who are they? What colors would best express the person you've decided to illustrate? Are they wealthy? Poor? Loud?

Thoughtful? Do they work in a position of hard labor or seek ways to avoid work at all costs? How old are they? What part of the world are they from?

Each question that you answer may only ever live within your mind, but that is part of the process. Enjoy it. And if you're using the Hand of Fate system and you don't like the results . . . go ahead and toss them out the window and start over. For more questions, go to section **W1** to peruse some of my favorites.

This is the power that you wield in telling these tales with your hobby choices.

Setting Your Palette

So assuming that you've either followed along with my instructions to this point or that you've skipped to this section and have already determined how you wish to paint your Knight of the Myth Vale, then at this point you should have in front of you a small collection of colors and all the tools that you need to move forward, ready to be put into service.

I typically put white on one end and black on the other and lay out each tone from light to dark, more or less. I know other painters adhere to a strict representation of the color wheel and others just drop the paint into a wholly unorganized mess. Use the process that works best for you and experiment with different methods until you are comfortable and able to move quickly among the paints that you have selected.

I do recommend that you keep your initial colors in a place that allows you to mix in a somewhat convenient area but prevents cross contamination.

Another thing to note when managing your painting palette real estate is to be aware of potential disasters when placing highly volatile and powerful shades next to the subtler and softer colors. Nothing can set you back quicker than when your red paint bleeds into the white or yellow at an unwanted moment.

Granted, this happens most often when using a wet palette, but if you are able to space these colors out a bit, you'll be setting yourself up for success and avoiding an accidental orange moment.

In between each color usage, be sure to thoroughly clean your brush. When using a variety of paints over a long painting session, be sure to change out your cleaning water from time to time. Personally, I keep two cups at hand when working: one to clean normal acrylic paints, the other for strictly metallic and other more complex paints, to prevent the flakes and other material that certain paints use from contaminating the other colors. In fact, I like to have a small bottle of clean water from which I draw all the water that I use in shining my paints.

At this point, go ahead and put a small amount of each color on your palette—whichever style that you've chosen to utilize—in an array that leads you across the scheme that you have in mind.

If you are already planning on mixing multiple tones of green but will be using a blue rarely, plan accordingly as you allot each paint its place on your palette. A little foresight here can make your job easier and more efficient.

Basic Acrylic Paint Consistency

With the paint shaken fully and applied to our working surface in a way that makes sense to us, the next piece of the puzzle is to ensure proper hydration and thickness.

As mentioned here and in likely every piece of miniature painting instruction in existence that predates the Neolithic era of the 1990s, water down your paints.

I'm guessing that you've heard that. If not, I'm honored to be the first to tell you.

Water down your paints.

However, while this is very true, in theory, the truth of the matter is a different story. To you, now, at the risk of creating some minor confusion in the short term but banking on the positive returns that this clarity will deliver in the future, I say:

Water down your paints . . . sometimes.

I wouldn't be doing you any great service if I told you that every time you put paint on your miniature, you will need to add X amount of water to get the best blend or the smoothest application.

The reality of the situation is that it just doesn't work that way.

There are some helpful things to keep in mind as you work and as you experience the process of painting and learn about the quality of your specific hobby products. With a little guidance here, I think that you'll unravel a system of the paint-to-water ratio that works best for you.

The truth is that every miniature paint on the market has strengths and weaknesses, and people choose to use one product over the other strictly because they prefer the way that the paint behaves. How you thin down a paint depends on the paint in question. Each paint has a different composition, age, and temperature, and other external factors that can affect the thickness of the paint.

Perhaps the paint on your palette is the right consistency directly out of the dropper or pot; maybe it isn't. So how do you know? First, let's determine a good baseline for comparison: heavy cream. Not whipped cream or any nonsense like that—we're talking about pushing your paints, generally speaking, to the consistency of plain old coffee cream. If you are unaware of what that looks like, I've included some helpful and wasteful photographs to ease your mind and illuminate you on the entire point of this particular discourse.

In sections **R2** I have listed some resources that may help you make some informed choices in the future. But as I've already stated, stick to one of the commercially available workhorse brands, and I'll give you the basic know-how about how to navigate the material during our early endeavors here.

Heavy cream has a body to it that regular milk lacks. It has a good deal of water in it, but, for the most part, it is thick enough to remain opaque until you spread it out to the furthest reaches of its ability to pool—then it has a transparency to it. When we paint, the goal is to start with a material that transfers as much pigment as possible without obscuring detail.

That's the real key—not obscuring detail and applying the most color possible. Now, as we continue to thin our paints, we begin to open the door to blending techniques that allow us to push colors along in tone and hue or even shift between colors in a gradient that is fully reliant on our ability and patience with thin layers of paint.

This is the first step in approaching those skills. Learn it well.

Let's keep exploring our paint at this stage and learn about how best to maintain consistency.

For the model in front of us, our stalwart Knight of the Myth Vale, we are seeking to apply clean and clear levels of paint that form a solid, clear base for us to build upon in later stages. Don't worry initially about weathering and details that you may have in mind for the finished product; focus instead on achieving a consistent application of paint across each of the dominant sections of the figure.

In the future, layering and blending will give you some creative methods that may not strictly follow the idea of painting the basic sections of the model in a single pass before moving forward into the next stages. And—like so many of the things that we do in the hobby—there are few rules and many pathways that can lead you to further growth and discovery.

For now, keep applying clear and clean full layers of each color.

When applying your colors, whatever they may be, be careful with your brushstrokes and don't be concerned if the primer is still exposed after you apply a thin layer of paint. This is to be expected. Once the first layer is fully dried, go back and apply a second coat. By now, you shouldn't necessarily see any primer, and the color should be fairly strong.

Now, as mentioned in the section on priming, **Quest II**, the difference in the color of primer that you chose will affect this. Black is much more difficult to cover than white. Still, with two or three thin coats, you should have a clear, strong tone that may have a little extra weight in it as a result of the choice that we've made to use black primer on the Knight of Myth Vale. As you'll learn, gray and white primer have their own benefits to brightness and vibrancy. They also bring their own challenges.

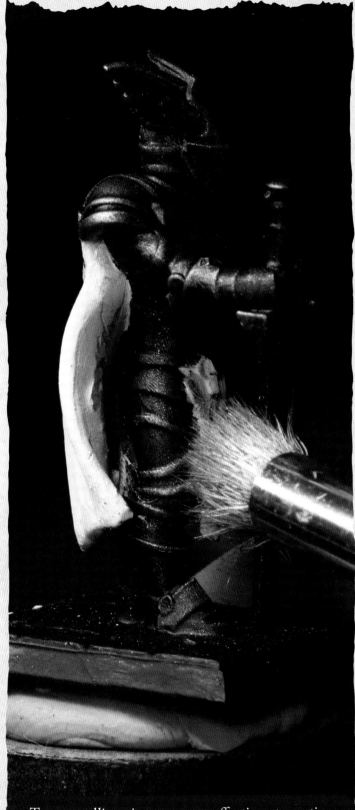

True metallic paints are very effective at creating a realistic metallic sheen that holds just enough reflectivity that we feel as though we are looking at steel, gold, or a wide variety of types of metal.

TRUE METALLIC ACRYLIC PAINTS

When painting with true metallics, there are some additional considerations. While we've been working with our pure-hue, traditional acrylic paint colors, if we decide to use any paints that contain the properties of true metallic paint, then we need to take some precautions to prevent contamination of our other paint, the water that we are using to clean our brushes, and the miniature itself.

Metallic paint contains microscopic flecks that create a glitter-like sheen that allows those shiny silvers, golds, coppers, and brasses to give the illusion of the reflectivity of actual metal. It isn't real metal at all.

Those flecks, while perfect for giving us an easy-to-use tool for creating the illusion of steel and gold, are a nightmare when they separate and get where you don't want them. If you've ever used glitter in any form of crafting, then you will already have experienced—in a macro setting—the same sort of consequence that metallic paint creates.

Metallic paints are best used on a hard palette, tile, plate, or any solid surface. If you do utilize a wet palette, you may find that the mica flakes migrate into all of your colors or the paint may separate more quickly than you want. This isn't the end of the world, but I prefer to err on the side of caution and use a solid palette.

You'll need a completely separate cup of water to rinse and clean your brush in, and you'll definitely not want to put it onto your wet palette if you have chosen to use one. Keep it safely separate from the other paints and be sure to really clean your brush after using it with any sort of metallic.

The Kobold Caverns are hidden close....

It is clear to you, after a few long moments of standing at the stone and dirt wall of the tavern cellar, that you are at a dead end. Your search has revealed very little other than the old rusted armor suit and more rats and cobwebs than you'd care to remember.

Painting the illusion of metal using techniques such as nonmetallic metal (known as NMM by the hobby community) is much more time consuming and requires a great deal of practice. It also comes with its own set of complications. We'll explore it, and some shortcuts that I utilize, in later sections of this book, but it is worth noting here, as it relates directly to the style of painting and color choices that we make in our initial planning and base coating.

Even though you should be shaking and mixing all of your paints, it becomes doubly important in the use of any true metallic paints. If necessary, stir the pot with a toothpick. Be certain to blend all the sedimented mica that invariably ends up settling at the bottom of the paint container. You'll find that most true metallic paints have a startlingly fast rate of separation. Be vigilant.

Every manufacturer has different compositions for their metallics, and, as such, they operate in wildly different ways. Spend the time to get to know the properties of the material that you have on hand.

✚ Metallics, as with flat base coats, can require two or more coats and should be thinned in much the same matter. In fact, metallics—in my experience—are often far thicker than flat acrylic colors.

✚ Move the model as needed, keeping your brush and motions consistent. Here the handle is very helpful in allowing for flexibility and control. It saves your miniature from smudging.

✚ When preparing for the true metallic gold, we are going to lay out an undercoat of a deep, rich brown. This technique works well to warm and slightly shift gold, brass, and copper metallics. You can use a variety of underpainting to produce a variety of effects; this will be your first!

✚ Different elements on any model will have different textures. For now, simply work to add a clean, clear base coat to each of the major areas. There will be plenty of time to expand on it.

✚ Turning the model around by the handle, work to fill in the major areas of interest on the model and alter your position and grip as needed, moving the model and your brush as one.

When it comes to keeping paint pots and dropper bottles well mixed and prepared for use, you can add stainless-steel ball bearings into each of your containers. These "agitators" can help to ensure that the paint is evenly dispersed throughout the entire body.

Ratios for Paint Thinning

(Paint to Water)

3:1 – Base

1:3 – Wash

1:4 – Glaze

Thinning your paints is not something that is easy to explain because of the wide difference in the quality and consistency of all of the many available products on the market. But as we've explored the subject fairly well at this point, I feel confident that we can discuss some generalized measurements that you can use as a set of guidelines in your work.

For every number of drops of paint, add the listed number of drops of clean water from an eyedropper. Again, these are general guidelines, but, hopefully, they will help you in your first experiments.

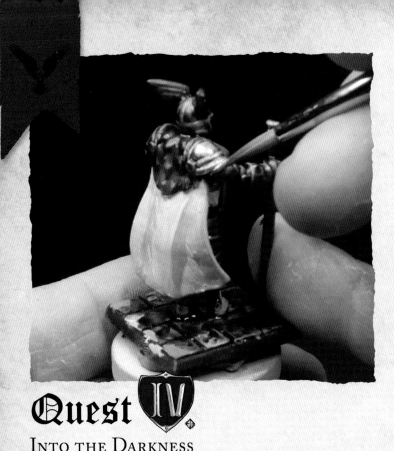

Quest IV
Into the Darkness

Washes, Shading, and Quick Shades

There is nothing mystical or baffling about the process of utilizing washes and shades in your painting work. It is a simple way to increase contrast and accomplish a lot of depth using quick techniques that require only a little know-how and some practice. In this Quest, you'll be armed with the knowledge that you need to accomplish a quick shade that brings depth and interest to your base coats.

As with our efforts in **Quest III**, washing and the use of shades come down to building a familiarity with your chosen tools and materials. Through practicing the application of these techniques on a variety of surface textures, you will learn how to replicate a variety of effects that can greatly improve the results of your miniature project.

For our purposes here, the use of "washing" and "shading" is defined as the following: the use of thinned paints and inks to create contrast by darkening the recesses of the model while leaving the more raised portions of the model brighter than those deeper areas. Washing is less controlled than shading.

Because of the thin consistency of the material used, the process creates a shorthand to what could amount to hours of lining and shading in a more controlled layer-painting technique.

Contrary to popular thought, you do not need to drench your model in a wash to use it in your painting routines. In fact, when I use washes, I rarely coat the entire figure and restrain my application to the specific area that I am working on at the time, in a darker tone of the color that I base coated that area in.

Glazing Overview

As for the exact number of applications, the thinner the wash is, the more control you possess in the effect that you create, and the more time you'll be spending on that work. It is essential, in any iteration of washing, to allow the previous layer of wash to fully and completely dry before applying a second, third, or fourth coat (ad infinitum). Otherwise, you risk the material drying in ugly tide pools and other strangeness that can ruin your hard work!

When you thin a paint down beyond the roughly 3:1 golden ratio, you start dealing with what is referred to as a glaze. (Once again, as mentioned elsewhere, consistency and material will always determine the correct ratios for each dilution.) *Glazing is the repeated use of extremely diluted paint in adding subtle characteristics and shifts in tone and hue to a base coat.* Like a shade, a glaze will tend to seek out the deeper recesses of a model and leave the higher points less affected. You will want to work to perfect your ability to place the watery material onto the area of your choice, learning to control each application.

With the right applications, you can use glazes to smooth out the stepped results of layer painting and create realistic skin tones and effects on a variety of materials that require a certain sense of translucency that opaque paints are incapable of providing. For a full exploration of the handling of skin tone, leather, and other organic materials of a wide variety of colors, you may wish to travel to **Quest X** to delve deeper into the subject. We, however, have plenty to discover here as we continue our discourse on the fundamentals of using washes and glazes in your miniature work. . . .

PREPARING FOR SIMPLE SHADING

In working our **Knight of the Myth Vale**, we will approach our use of washes and shades in a controlled, careful manner, but we are going to work in larger areas quickly enough to accomplish our work efficiently.

✢ When working with the Knight of the Myth Vale, in examining the major segments of the model, we find that we can separate them into three portions and shade them each accordingly.

✢ When working with shades, remember to let each layer dry before moving on to the next.

✢ (There are plenty of reasons and techniques in our future lessons that will allow you to play fast and loose with the dry time of your paint, but in these exercises, we are best served by a patient and measured approach. Stick to allowing these layers the necessary dry time!)

✢ With this knight, the three primary segments of interest are the cloak and tabard, the shield, and the armor itself.

✢ The armor is the primary center of focus for any knight, regardless of creed or house.

Each of these items could be quickly shaded using a single dark-tone wash that is evenly spread across the surface of the model, but while quick and fully acceptable, that approach would leave a dirty and flat result that—unless you are looking for that appearance or are compromising your approach to facilitate speed—will dull the overall contrast of the base coat and faintly filter all of your previous work in the dark tone used.

There are specialty products on the market that work exactly this way, and you can produce acceptable to good results with quick, whole-miniature dips—but with some slight additions to the techniques that you use and the time that you invest in this stage of work, you can easily produce effects that quickly bring your completed effort to a much more professional-looking standard.

I've included some information on dip washing in the later sections of **Quest XI** and in the resource listings in section **R1**, should you be more interested in batch painting—quickly and effectively—leaving more delicate artistic concerns roundly in the dirt.

(And given the scope of army painting, no one will fault you for taking as many shortcuts as are available to you, for as a hobbyist, all too often our eyes are bigger than our free time, and much of our collection sits collecting dust in "Piles of Shame," mocking us eternally.)

models is to start working from the lowest layer up—or, more clearly, to shade and wash the deeper segments of the miniature and work my way up to the light tones and higher areas.

On this model, that means that we will start on the armor with a deeper dark tone. I'm using a premade product here; however, you can easily mix your own washes by properly watering down your acrylic paints. But, again, such work can be tricky and requires an experienced eye to produce results that are neither too thick nor too watery. Tide marks can be left on your work if you are not careful in your application.

The dark tone is applied liberally but in a controlled manner on the recessed areas of the knight's armor. Anything that I've base coated in a metallic is receiving this treatment. Depending on the subtlety of the result that you are seeking, you could apply multiple thin coats, allowing each to dry before proceeding with the next. In this case, I'm applying two fairly heavy passes of the dark tone but keeping the tip of the brush focused on the separations between each of the plates of armor and the areas where the armor meets another material or color.

When the armor dark tone wash is fully dry, we can move onto the tabard and the cloak. The pale blue wash that I created here is extremely thin and—while I still have applied only two fairly thick coats—much the same as our previous work with the armor. I find that different materials require different approaches to the use of your brush. Here I followed the flow of the fabric and gently drew my brush across the deep folds of the cloak and fabric portions of the garb. The highest points I've avoided entirely, leaving the base coat untouched. The deepest areas are receiving the majority of the tone; in between the high and the low, I'm carefully blending out lighter applications.

For the shield, in this example, I've mixed a deeper green wash and am focusing the use of it to the crevices and edges that separate the metal rim from the flat enameled surface of the front of the shield. In addition to that, to add some volume we can blend up some of the darker tone on the bottom third of the shield.

Shade selection and application for this exercise: a dark tone of brown or black wash can be used on the armor alongside a darker tone of whichever hue was chosen for the shield. For the cloak and tabard, you can also shade with a darker tone of the base coat that you used or—in the example that I've provided here—a pale blue.

Shading and painting white are subjects fully deserving of their own discussions, so you can explore those topics in greater detail in **Quest VIII**. The advanced techniques will be available to you there and learning to correctly approach white and black will give you a great advantage in all of your future painting, but for this Quest, know that using a pale blue on the whites will provide you with an adequate result.

Much like when painting our base coats, order of operation is a matter of preference. That said, my preference for most

The wax candle in your hand flickers in the darkness of the musty air, and the smell of sour wine and wet earth permeates this portion of the tavern cellar. Above you, the old wooden board creaks as patrons and the tavern keeps move about. The faint sound of a poorly tuned mandolin can be heard—thankfully muffled—through the thick rotting wood planks. Still, according to the cryptic notes of the map, the entryway into the caverns should be hidden somewhere close by.

Roll 1 D4 (a single four-sided die). There may not be may options on this die, but you should know that even the humble D4 has great power when used within The Hand of Fate system to determine your painting choices. . . .

1	You have spent far too many days days in the far lands and dungeons of the world beyond the borders of your homeland. You have become a stranger in your own home and carry your entire life on your back. Your equipment and armor are more worn and your cloak more tattered than those of your sibling knights. You have seen much and look the part of a vagabond.
2	Having studied at the greatest libraries in the many realms of the land, you are astute and careful in your actions. You prefer to study rather than rollick in a tavern in your spare time. Your appearance is organized and befits a knight of learning. Your gear is laden with books and your fingers often bear the ink stains of a scribe. You believe that the pen is indeed mightier than the sword, but you have a blade that you are well trained in . . . just in case.
3	Roses, roses everywhere. Flowers are your trade and you are more happy with fresh dirt between your fingers than a bloodied blade. You can't possibly imagine a life without a garden of some sort and are happiest when you are out in the wild places of the world. Your comrades in arms often say that you should have been a ranger, and perhaps they are correct. With your armor emblazoned with small flourishes that mark your passion for roses and wild growth, you have lovingly painted thorns and leaves across your garb.
4	To you, the sound of coins jingling in a purse is like the music of the fairest kind. You are not greedy or deceptive in your trade, but as a knight, you are not against the tribute of those that you faithfully serve. Measuring your deeds in the ledgers that you fastidiously keep as you travel through the cities and fields of the land is your great pleasure. The signs of your wealth might be subtle or clear, but your gear is well maintained and of fine make, as you can afford the best of the best.

Determine some of the backstory that best represents your knight and use the results to make decisions in your themes and color choices.

As always and ever, feel free to wildly and creatively elaborate on what Fate determines here.

✠ Often misrepresented in the past, darkened history of the hobby, **washes** have been thought of as a full and complete coat that is slathered across a miniature indiscriminately.

✠ When utilizing **washes** and **glazes**, you can expedite your work by keeping a hair dryer close at hand while you work.

✠ It is quite important to allow a wash coat to fully and completely dry before moving forward and adding additional layers or washes, highlights, or glazes. A hair dryer can help to speed your work and improve the quality of work by preventing muddy results.

There are a large number of prepared wash and shade products on the market. Some are acrylic; some are enamel and oil based. While we will certainly delve into the secrets and magic of using more than simple acrylic paints, we won't be doing so until we are significantly further along in this journey together.

✠ As always, feel free to jump ahead to **Quest XI** to learn more or peruse the resources discussed in the appendixes, but be forewarned: the materials in those techniques require special care and consideration when used.

And while they absolutely produce wonderful and speedy results, if misused, they can create huge problems for a beginner painter.

Travel forth at your own risk. For those of you who plan to walk the road here, let's continue onward. . . .

Quest V

ILLUMINATED GLORY

HIGHLIGHTING

Once the shading and washing of our knight are behind us and the model has fully dried, we can see that we have darkened much of the model, our original base-coating work has been brought down, and the contrast on the model is beginning to take shape. This is the point that we begin to replicate the highlights that will create even more depth and build the illusion that light is striking the model.

With that progress in mind, the next step that we will examine is the use of painting highlights that create the representation of light touching upon the highest, most visible sections of the figure. This process is the polar opposite of the previous steps. Where we used shade to darken, we must now use lighter paints to increase the illusion of illumination and bring our model that much closer to completion.

There are a few simple ways to accomplish this. The three that we will be exploring are layer painting, edge highlighting, and dry brushing. Each has strengths, and each has weaknesses. Their use is determined by the need of the model and your desired outcome. Once we define the styles and results of each, you'll be able to determine which technique best serves your needs and desires.

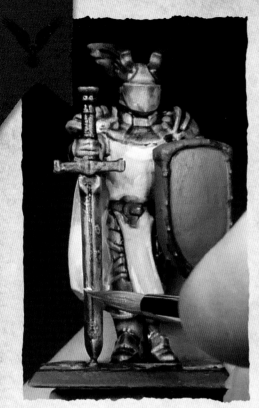
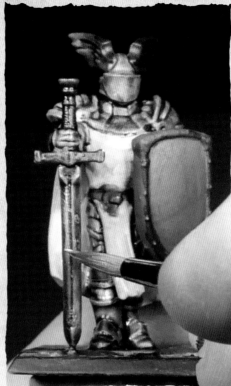

Layer Highlighting

Layer highlighting (also known as layer painting) not only is functional in the application of highlights on a model but also can incorporate shading just as easily. Here, in this discussion, we focus on using the method of stacking the paint in successively smaller strokes to build a gradually stepped transition between light and dark. Most of the time, this will mean that your darker layers will be placed first, followed by your mid-tones, and completed with the highest points of the model painted with the last layers in much thinner, smaller sections that are laid down on the highest levels.

This Quest will serve to add a few highlights, building on our core base coat colors and lightening them with the use of hues that are similar but lighter to produce the illusion of light striking the model at the highest points. We can mix a little white into the original color, but that will also desaturate the color, making it more subdued in vibrancy. For simplicity's sake, find a color that is slightly brighter than your base and use that in this section. On the shield, I've used a slightly lighter green and applied it to only about 50 percent of the surface.

Knowing where and how to apply these layers is a matter of practice, but a general rule of thumb is to imagine a light source, like the sun, striking your miniature and applying the lighter-color paints to only the area that would be illuminated.

If you need some help imagining that, hold your miniature under a desk lamp and turn off all other lights. Move it around to see the varied effects of the directional light.

You can continue to use lighter and lighter paints in these layers to create amazingly nuanced finishes.

Edge Highlighting

Edge highlighting is a style that paints the highest brightness of a hue on the sharpest edges of the model, creating a reverse lining of highlight that brings sharp contrast to the newly shaded dark areas. The illusion of depth is created, and the model becomes more visibly dynamic at a distance and improves our showing on a game table.

I often use the side of my brush in the execution of this technique. I patiently move the brush carefully around the sharp edges and highest points of the miniature, while avoiding the shading and base-coat work that I've already completed.

As with the layer-painting technique above, you will want to use a lighter shade of your original base coat. Sometimes white is the correct choice here, but it is rare that I use it in edge highlighting unless I am, in fact, highlighting a white object. If you want the stark power of white, consider using an off-white, either warm or cool.

If you'd like to learn about painting with white and black, or color theory in general, you can find a wealth of information in the special Side Quest after **Quest VII**.

When edge highlighting, you don't want a very thick line of your chosen color, just a sharp and crisp line that works all along your model in various sections of material.

You can even create texture in the way that you apply the highlight. Try painting a more jagged and broken line to create a sense of aging and texture. On armor, this would read as dents and dings, a battle-worn suit of metal that has seen better days. On fabric, it would look like the edges of the material were tattered and torn.

Experiment with the technique and see what sort of effects you can create.

Dry Brushing

Dry brushing is less controlled than the previous two options, but it is a technique that can be used effectively to quickly and easily produce dramatic results with minimum effort. It requires a few special items that allow for the effect to work. First, a painter will require a flat brush that is strong enough to take a beating but gentle enough to have a bend that facilitates the transfer of paint to the miniature.

In my personal work, I have found that inexpensive and small makeup brushes are the best option and easily replaced again and again. Do not attempt to dry brush with any brush that you are not completely fine with relegating to this task and this task alone.

Dry brushing is endlessly destructive to the brushes used. The results that you can achieve, however, make the use of it essential in most early hobby experimentation and discovery. Some artists prefer to avoid it entirely, as without extreme care, the technique is sloppy and can bleed onto other segments of the model. It can appear chalky and dull if done incorrectly and without an eye to brush control and the exercise of patience.

✝ By dipping your brush into undiluted paint, you are seeking to break all of the rules that you've been told up to this point in regard to the use and care of your brush. A dry brush—either a makeup brush or an artist's brush—is going to be destroyed. Fill the tip of the brush with paint, then immediately begin to remove that paint by rubbing it against a surface that removes the paint to the point that you can no longer see the paint on the brush.

✝ Then, working carefully and patiently, draw the seemingly clean brush against the model in a single direction as you begin picking out the raised surfaces. You can mix an escalating color scheme that brings the contrast to powerful and simple results.

Dry brushing can do wonders to quickly and effectively help you to render fur, feathers, hair, and other highly textured areas with impressive results. Just as with all of our previous techniques, dry brushing works best when you add multiple lighter shades of your original base coat to the model in successive layers from dark to light.

The temptation to simply use white in this method is understandable but is a mistake if not used for a specific purpose. Again, use a slightly lighter shade and work your way up. White does have its uses and creates a powdery, aged finish, but that is a specific result for specific purposes.

The downside of chalky finishes is very much minimized when white is taken out of the equation. Take your time and build up your effect by removing as much paint as possible from your brush. It really does work best when you use less material.

It is not uncommon to use two or more of these techniques together in the completion of your painting work. Each of these styles is a tool, and the outcome of each provides you with a specific means to create the illusion of light upon the model and gives you the ability to determine the mood and look of the final piece.

The Escape from the Kobold Caverns

How long did you stumble, wet and cold, through the dank caverns beneath the World's Edge Mountains? A day? A full ten days? Perhaps more?

The map was true, and the strange old man hadn't lied to you: it led you to what you were seeking, the Eye of Wonder. And now that the gem—brightly shimmering in your hands—is yours, you can't help but smile at the very real possibility that you may not make it out of this place alive.

You aren't sure what the kobolds had coated their spears with, but your shoulder is horribly inflamed from your wound, and the minor cuts on your legs and back burn as if on fire. Your head swims, and the world fades in and out of focus as you march onward in the dark, hoping for some sign of escape from this maze of rock and mire.

You wanted an adventure, but you hadn't anticipated that the cost would be so high. Mayhaps your family was right and a simple life of work and toil would be better suited to your needs.

You have only a single tinder twig left, but you won't waste it until you find something—anything—dry enough to burn and make a torch from. Your head continues to spin drunkenly as you splash forward. Either the kobolds have given up on chasing you down or they are waiting for their poisons to take full effect before catching you up in their sharp spend nets. Perhaps they know that you won't make it very far with your stolen treasure here in this twisted collection of passages and caverns.

For a moment you think that you are hallucinating. As you stumble farther down the rocky cavern, you see before you an old weaver's wheel, broken and covered in cobwebs. It is lit by a thin shaft of moonlight that strikes down upon it from a jagged gap in the cave ceiling. You run your hand across the rotten wood wheel to prove to yourself that it is real. Crawling up, you discover that you have walked far, indeed, and have emerged into the ruins of an old stone keep, the broken remains of some forgotten and remote homestead once belonging to some far-flung noble, living on the edge of the civilized world out here. . . . It's no inn, and covered in spiders and dust, but it will serve you well for the night and—after your recent encounters—is a welcome and beautiful sight.

In the following pages, you'll find a custom map of the **ruined estate**. Feel free to pull it out of this guidebook and use it in your own tabletop games!

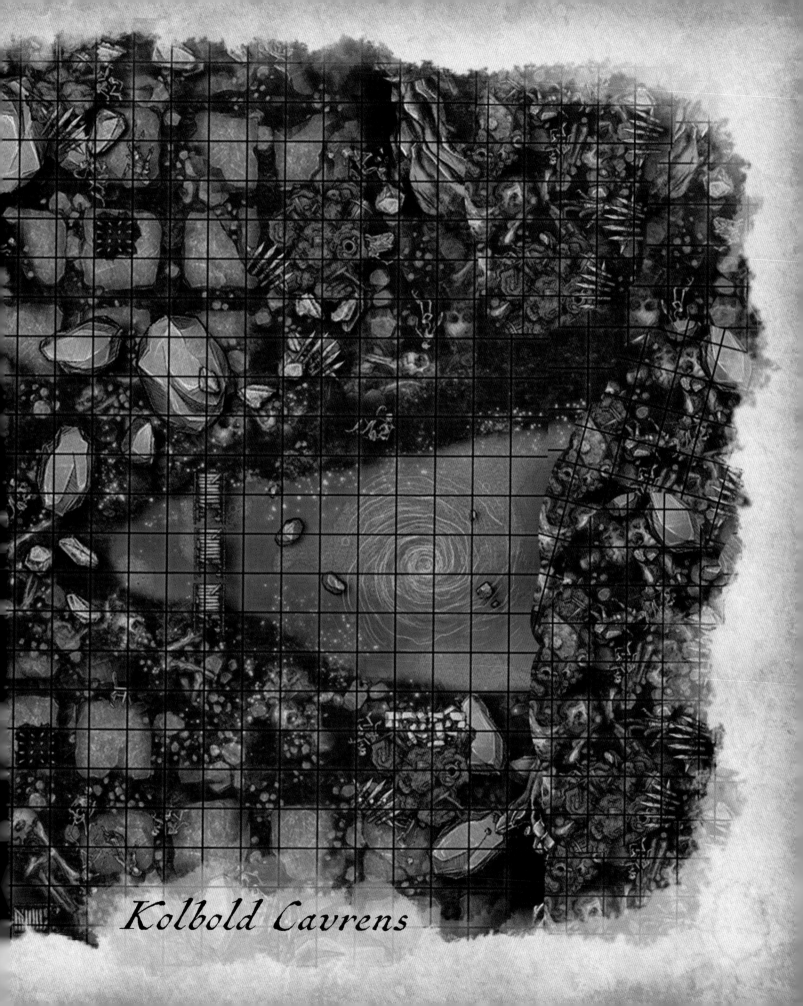

Kolbold Cavrens

Quest VI

Sealing Fate

Sealants and Varnishes

When you have finished the hours of work that you have lavished upon your chosen model, after you have lovingly applied the base coats, created dynamic contrast through the careful application of washes and shade, and sharpened the visual impact with highlights and layering, it stands to reason that you would—likely—prefer that your small work of art not be chipped and worn to an unappealing smudge of ruined paint and wasted effort.

Varnishes and sealants are the most effective tools in protecting your hard work. In this section of our guidebook, we are going to explore your options.

Should you opt to leave your figure in its current state, without a protective coat of clear material to shield it, you will discover that your work will inevitably require some corrective repairs at some point in the future.

Such undertakings are rarely able to produce the best results and will require that you accept the reality that your original work will never fully be recaptured or preserved in its entirety.

The use of any varnish or sealer is typically applied by one of three popular means. I shall—of course—give you what guidance I can here but will do so with all of the warnings that such products should have attached to their use.

Types of Sealants and Application

You can apply matte, gloss, or satin varnishes with a brush—though I would strongly suggest that you use inexpensive and less than cherished brushes when coating your model in such thick material.

Any varnish can wreck an expensive brush quickly. It is also meant to dry hard and form a protective shell that is both clear and strong. In your brush, if not removed, that spells out doom and destruction.

Alternatively, rather than relying on brushwork, you can opt to call upon any of the commercially available rattle-can spray lacquers that remove the need for you to ruin brushes or learn complicated machinery such as an airbrush. Any such spray work requires that you prepare for the use of these products and protect yourself against the harmful vapors that are produced in their usage. A correctly fitted mask that is properly rated for protection against fumes and particulate sprays is essential and should still be used even outside or in an extremely well-ventilated space.

Sprays can help you to quickly and effectively coat your model in a thin, transparent layer of varnish that, once dry, prevents any further work needed to protect your painting. But they create harmful environmental conditions that you should avoid and protect yourself against.

While I cannot expound upon the full usage of the tool in this section, the airbrush is the most advanced—and difficult—method of application. The use of this tool could easily fill a tome of this size twice over, but I have included some basic instruction and information in section **R3** and in later Quests.

When using an airbrush to varnish, much like aerosol sprays, you are able to apply a very thin and efficient coat of whatever sheen of varnish that you've chosen.

Airbrushes, however, are not for the casual or inexperienced hobbyist. They are expensive, require a great deal of maintenance, and are prone to complications that can fully and completely negate the benefits of their use.

For our work—and in keeping with our pledge to explore the simplest and most straightforward techniques of the hobby—I am applying a matte varnish with a number 2 synthetic hairbrush that I spent less than $2 on. Rather than spreading varnish on the hard palette or—worse—the wet palette, I find that keeping and collecting a selection of medicine measuring cups, small ramekin containers, and other little vessels allows me to manage and control my varnish applications without making a large and unruly mess.

Once all of the previous work is fully and completely dry, I apply a few thin coats of the varnish over the entirety of the miniature, using a series of strokes that follow the general flow and motion of the model.

Blend the edges of each stroke together and work slowly enough to prevent pooling on any of the recesses or folds of the sculpt.

Once varnish dries, it cannot be easily removed, and while you can strip the entire model, you are restricted to forward momentum after taking this step. I often paint over varnish. You'll likely find reasons to seal your work and

then add additional techniques. Some future tricks will require it.

It is worth exploring the use of matte and gloss varnishes in washing or when halfway through a painting project to set certain layers. Once the underlying paint layers are set, the use of pigment powders and other elements such as oil washes is possible and easier to manipulate.

Once sealed, allow the miniature to dry for a few hours and celebrate your achievement! You've completed the Path of the New Apprentice! Trade in the Raven Rucksack at Thaco Thistle-britches's Caravan and venture forth into the unknown as we begin to examine some new, more specific models and the challenges that they pose!

A Color Theory Side Quest

Perhaps the most challenging part of painting miniatures is determining the colors that you choose to use in each of your works. It can be daunting to face a bare, primed figure that is waiting patiently to be brought to life under your brush. The choices are nearly endless and will tell stories in your selections and placement. And while there are exercises that can help to expand your abilities, the best way to improve your eye is to study other artwork—both miniature hobby art and traditional art—and to consider what makes your favored pieces attractive.

Creativity is a skill, not a talent. It may be something that certain individuals are naturally more prone to but because it is a skill, it is something that anyone can improve their ability to utilize. Much of what we consider good taste or dynamic design is the careful combination of colors, shapes, and textures selected by an artist who has spent countless hours honing their eye. Color selection may seem simple and intuitive—and it can be—but such choices are carefully made and are informed by a few principles that can be learned and developed, just like brushwork and paint application.

One of the crucial elements that will assist you in this journey is the use and understanding of the color wheel. The wheel itself is simple, but mastering it requires more work and copious experimentation.

✛ Color theory is the practical combination of our understanding of how colors compliment and contrast each other. An ancient wizard known as Isaac Newton is—to the best of our knowledge—the first to have mapped the color spectrum in a wheel. The relationship between all of the varied colors can be understood and directed through the use of a color wheel, many examples of which have been included here in this guide for you to utilize in the work that you will undertake in choosing the schemes for your models.

In the wider world of the Inter-Web, you can find any number of fantastic tutorials that will instruct you on the basics of painting models and miniatures, converting, and kitbashing—and I'm thankful for it—but I feel that the discussion and exploration of the more academic elements of color usage and storytelling are often missing.

It is my hope that you will find the following Side Quest helpful and informative: a review for some of you, perhaps, or fresh and new to others. Regardless of on which side of that divide you stand, it is in the spirit of exploration that we move forward and examine the uses and power of the color wheel!

This discussion is the quickest way for you to improve the results of your hobby work. Understanding some of the classic "art room" education will give you the confidence to make informed choices and to focus the results of your visual storytelling as a painter and hobbyist.

Let's begin by exploring the wide variety of terms that are commonly bantered about in the majority of conversations about color theory.

SCHEMES AND COMBINATIONS

Monotone is a scheme that utilizes a single neutral tone in varying tints and shades. Off-whites, beiges, grays, and taupes are examples of popular usages. The darkening and lightening of these elements may vary, but the overall scope of the scheme is as limited as it could possibly be.

Interestingly, the use of pure white is not monotone, as it is considered too brilliant. **Neutral tones** are those that are unobtrusive and subtle, but they are capable of expressing a wide variety of intention in the reduced scope of the limitation that a monotone scheme demands.

Warm and cool tones within the strictly wrangled constraints of the monotone palette can shift those tones to tell a story—if one that is less overt than a scheme that uses the full spread and diversity of the color wheel.

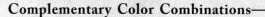

Monochromatic—Using a single hue or various tones of the same hue creates what is known as a monochromatic color scheme. Much like with a monotone scheme, the limitations of the usage of this palette can create dynamic and powerful results but—on the opposite end of the spectrum—can devolve into a bland and tedious visual delivery. A palette of all red or all violet, blue, or yellow is a strong statement. The choice has merit, if that is the impact that you are seeking to convey and if the miniature that you are painting can carry it.

Complementary Color Combinations—When we are seeking the most pronounced contrast and impact between colors, we look to the opposite side of the color wheel to pair a color with a partner that will generate a bright and elevated synergy between the two.

Color Combinations—These are where we find the widest possibility for discovering a language for us to use in communicating a story with our painting work. The way that we distribute those choices—the way that we interpose, layer, stack, and pair color—is one of the key skills that we can, and I argue should, consciously practice and hone through our years in the hobby.

Monochromatic Scheme—Using a number of tones, shades, and tints of the same hue, we create a more harmonious and unified palette that can allow more subtle results than those that are created through complementary combinations. We'll examine the specific reasons and uses of this sort of choice further in our adventures.

The properties of color can greatly affect the tone and mood of your work. Each shift in the vibrancy and hue creates a different emotional response, and we can relate a story to each accordingly. The fainter and more desaturated a hue is, the lighter and airier it seems; the darker a hue is, the more oppressed and weighty it can feel.

ANALOGOUS COLOR COMBINATIONS

Analogous Scheme—This consists of a triad of colors that are adjacent to each other on the color wheel. This combination creates a strong sense of uniformity and can be put to effective use in a variety of army lists and other large groups of miniatures that you wish to bear a clear association. This scheme works best when a single hue is selected to do the heavy lifting and as a dominant focus, with the other two colors working in support of it.

Triadic Scheme—A triadic scheme is defined by the triangular pattern that it uses to connect the colors on the color wheel. It creates a high-contrast combination that offers the painter a powerful, dynamic scheme that draws from a diverse pool of color. If you are not cautious, however, the colors may resolve themselves in a garish way. Experiment with tone and intensity to help lessen the visual impact.

Tetradic Scheme—While risking the balance between tones more than many of the other schemes, tetradic combinations take from a wide variety of colors from the color wheel due to the rectangular shape that overlays the choices available when using this method. As with many multicolor combinations, it behooves us to select a single focal color choice and then allow the other colors to settle into supporting roles for the star performer.

There are a few other definitions and elaborations that will aid us in our work and understanding of how color can be best used to create a scheme that expresses the meaning and story that we wish to convey.

Hue—Hue is best explained in the descriptions of any color on the color wheel and helps to determine the shifts between all of the colors available.

Value—Value is the lightness or darkness of a color and is directly tied to the grayscale that—without hue—moves between black and white. Luminance is another way to express this.

Intensity or Saturation—This is the purity of a color in relation to the value scale and the vibrancy of the hue. How close to an unaltered color is the selection?

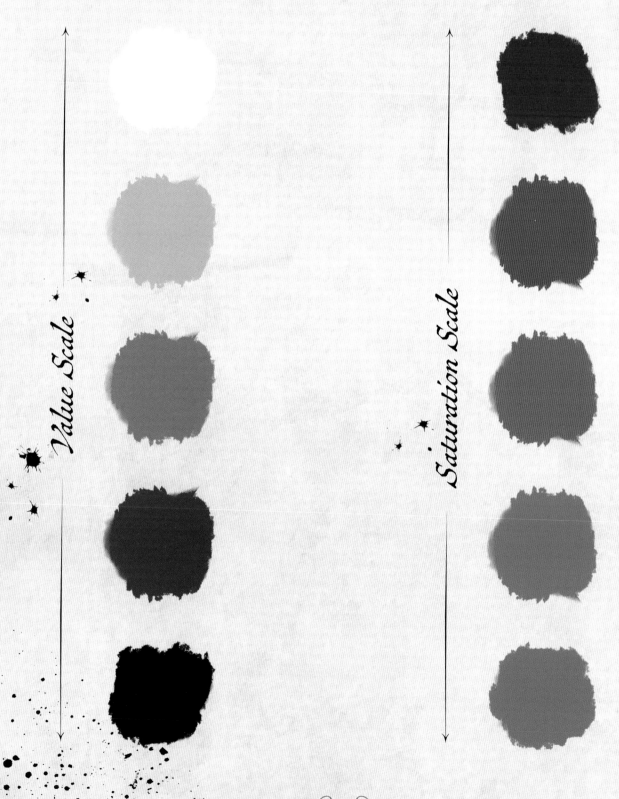

Value Scale

Saturation Scale

Tint—When white is introduced to the hue, it becomes a tint, as the bright whiteness draws the saturation and intensity out it, transforming it into a faded and airy color.

Shade—Much like a tint, a shade is the same process of desaturation, but it utilizes black rather than white. The hues created are dulled but in a way that is deeper in the expression of the hue—heavier and more substantial but lacking in the vibrancy of the original hue.

Tint Scale

Shade Scale

Key Color—The dominant hue in a scheme will maintain the largest amount of surface area in a composition. The other colors will bolster and support or contrast, but the dramatic effect that this choice has on your final piece cannot be overstated. Test this by painting similar models with the same three colors and alternate which of them is your key color.

THE COLOR WHEEL

There are two distinct types of color wheels, but each is based on the spectrum of color as our eyes perceive it.

The first type of color wheel is the **RYB**, which is most directly related to us in the sense that it is the traditional wheel used in mixing paint colors.

Any kindergartner would be able to recite to you the twelve main colors that find themselves on the RYB wheel and how they relate to one another: red, yellow, and blue as the primaries and all other tones mixing into the secondary and tertiary colors, orange, purple, green, red-orange, yellow-orange, yellow-green, blue-green, blue-violet, and red-violet.

An **RGB** color wheel, conversely, is tied to the way that light interacts with color. This typically is used in the applications that utilize computer or television screens.

Red, blue, and green are the primaries here, and cyan, magenta, and yellow are the secondaries. The tertiary colors in this set are orange, chartreuse green, spring green, azure, violet, and rose.

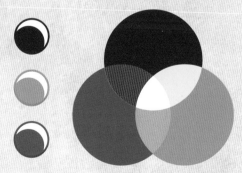

As mentioned earlier, our understanding of these spectrums of light was first discovered and explored by an ancient wizard named Sir Isaac Newton. His studies revealed that clear light is made from seven visible colors, and he codified his discovery in the acronym and spell-name of **ROYGBIV**.

Whenever you witness a rainbow, this magic becomes clear and quite apparent.

ROYGBIV = Red, Orange, Yellow, Green, Blue, Indigo, Violet

With this in mind, how can this knowledge assist us in creating exciting and powerful miniature studies in our hobby adventures?

The power of color truly comes from understanding the tension and tranquility that can be crafted from the choices that you as an artist can make to express emotion and story. I find that I repeat that often, but I feel that it really bears the duplication. Understand what colors can evoke and you'll improve your work exponentially in a very short amount of time.

In my experience—which, again, isn't endless and unblemished—a painter can carefully and cleanly apply base coats and work with some shading techniques to achieve results that are very much improved by a focused understanding of how to place colors in a way that draws and controls the way that the eye travels over the miniature.

If you are willing to invest in your skill set and spend days and weeks and years honing the techniques that you'll gather in your painting career, you'll find that at the very foundation of the process those choices and first base coats will do more to determine the look and style of your work than any amount of wet blending or object source lighting effects or edge highlighting.

Your core use of color and the choices that you make will define the lion's share of your results. Spending the time to examine the meanings and scientific use of every color asset available to you will position you for greater success in all of the advanced elements of the craft as they present themselves.

Let's begin a more in-depth usage of the idea of controlled color schemes and put them in direct practice. I'll continue to lay out the knowledge that I possess as I guide you along the way, and whether you are an experienced hobbyist or fresh from the village of Noob, I will do my best to arm you with something of interest and use!

On the page, you'll find a wheel that is focused not on the traditional balance of color but one that exhibits the positive and negative qualities that are traditionally associated with each of the colors, including white, black, and gray.

These descriptions are guidelines, not rules, but they may assist you in approaching the matter in a different mindset.

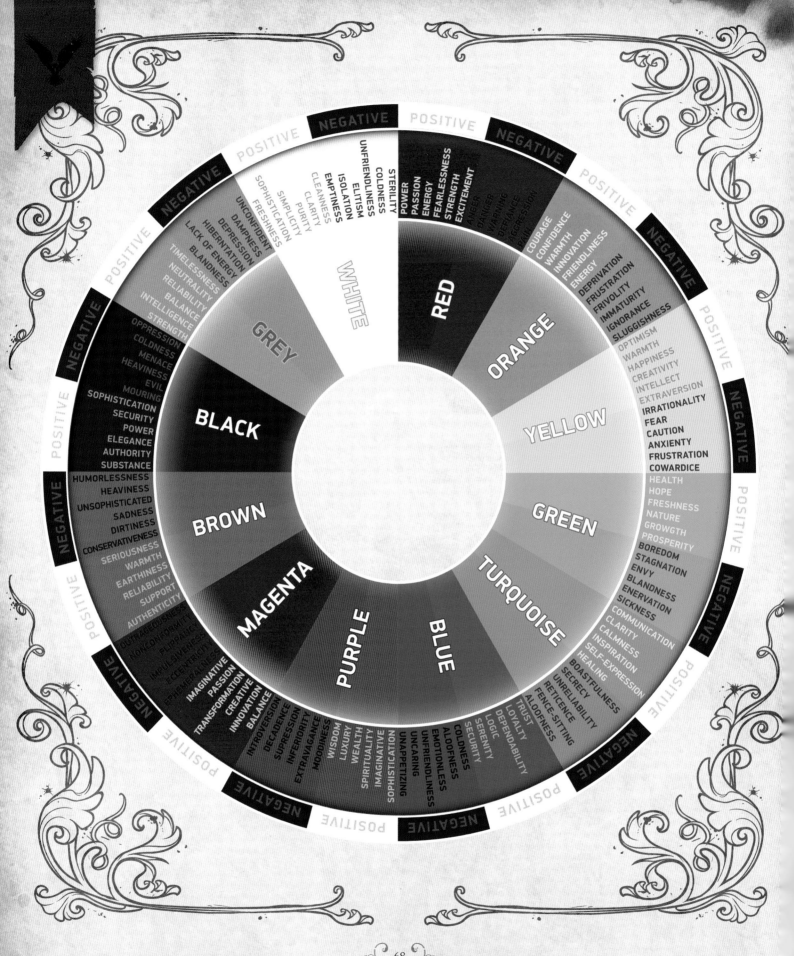

RED — NEGATIVE: ANGER, DANGER, WARNING, DEFIANCE, AGGRESSION, PAIN
RED — POSITIVE: POWER, PASSION, ENERGY, FEARLESSNESS, STRENGTH, EXCITEMENT

ORANGE — POSITIVE: COURAGE, CONFIDENCE, WARMTH, INNOVATION, FRIENDLINESS, ENERGY
ORANGE — NEGATIVE: DEPRIVATION, FRUSTRATION, FRIVOLITY, IMMATURITY, IGNORANCE, SLUGGISHNESS

YELLOW — POSITIVE: OPTIMISM, WARMTH, HAPPINESS, CREATIVITY, INTELLECT, EXTRAVERSION
YELLOW — NEGATIVE: IRRATIONALITY, FEAR, CAUTION, ANXIETY, FRUSTRATION, COWARDICE

GREEN — POSITIVE: HEALTH, HOPE, FRESHNESS, NATURE, GROWGTH, PROSPERITY
GREEN — NEGATIVE: BOREDOM, STAGNATION, ENVY, BLANDNESS, ENERVATION, SICKNESS

TURQUOISE — POSITIVE: COMMUNICATION, CLARITY, CALMNESS, INSPIRATION, SELF-EXPRESSION, HEALING
TURQUOISE — NEGATIVE: SECRECY, UNRELIABILITY, BOASTFULNESS, RETICENCE, FENCE-SITTING, ALOOFNESS

BLUE — POSITIVE: TRUST, LOYALTY, DEPENDABILITY, LOGIC, SERENITY, SECURITY
BLUE — NEGATIVE: COLDNESS, ALOOFNESS, EMOTIONLESS, UNFRIENDLINESS, UNCARING, UNAPPETIZING

PURPLE — POSITIVE: WISDOM, LUXURY, WEALTH, SPIRITUALITY, IMAGINATIVE, SOPHISTICATION
PURPLE — NEGATIVE: INTROVERSION, DECADENCE, SUPRESSION, INFERIORITY, EXTRAVAGANCE, MOODINESS

MAGENTA — POSITIVE: IMAGINATIVE, PASSION, TRANSFORMATION, CREATIVE, INNOVATION, BALANCE
MAGENTA — NEGATIVE: OUTRAGEOUSNESS, NONCONFORMITY, FLIPPANCY, IMPULSIVENESS, ECCENTRICITY, EPHEMERALNESS

BROWN — POSITIVE: SERIOUSNESS, WARMTH, EARTHINESS, RELIABILITY, SUPPORT, AUTHENTICITY
BROWN — NEGATIVE: HUMORLESSNESS, HEAVINESS, UNSOPHISTICATED, SADNESS, DIRTINESS, CONSERVATIVENESS

BLACK — POSITIVE: SOPHISTICATION, SECURITY, POWER, ELEGANCE, AUTHORITY, SUBSTANCE
BLACK — NEGATIVE: OPPRESSION, COLDNESS, MENACE, HEAVINESS, EVIL, MOURING

GREY — POSITIVE: TIMELESSNESS, NEUTRALITY, RELIABILITY, BALANCE, INTELLIGENCE, STRENGTH
GREY — NEGATIVE: UNCONFIDENT, HIBERNATION, DEPRESSION, DAMPNESS, LACK OF ENERGY, BLANDNESS

WHITE — POSITIVE: SOPHISTICATION, FRESHNESS, SIMPLICITY, PURITY, CLARITY, CLEANNESS
WHITE — NEGATIVE: STERILITY, COLDNESS, UNFRIENDLINESS, ELITISM, ISOLATION, EMPTINESS

Much art is based on the emotion and tone that the specific piece of art invokes. By studying the traditional associations with all of the colors, we can make choices—or break the rules and standards—with an informed color scheme that expresses the mood and emotion that you wish.

Rather than immediately telling you that certain combinations look good together and others don't, hopefully this examination will encourage you to think about what it is that you wish to imbue your work with. What emotion? What story? That is the true beginning of your work. The painting will come soon enough.

The primary colors exist in balance with secondary shades and tertiary hues between the primaries and secondaries. The best wheels have a few layers that you can rotate to see the results of mixing colors together.

The best place to begin when exploring the world of color theory is the color wheel. You'll find various versions of wheels in this section but also may find pocket color wheels at any art shop or even among the office supplies at most big-box retailers.

There are also countless online merchants who would likely be thrilled to have your business!

Color Meaning and Mood

Use the brief descriptions that are included below to fuel the flames of your curiosity and ensure that you do not allow your explorations to end there! Each definition and elaboration is a starting point and should not be seen as a mandate or ironclad interpretation. The perspectives of different people will always bring new and interesting viewpoints to meaning behind any color. Take what you like, leave the rest. . . .

Yellows—Warm and sunny, yellow offers a brightness that often speaks of positive and hopeful vibrations of bold energy. Optimism and uplifting positivity are often linked to the hue, but as with all colors, how it is used and the colors paired with it make all the difference. Paired with black, it becomes heightened and brings a sense of danger and striking aggression.

Red—This color is full of intensity and speaks of wealth and power. Its relation to sacrifice and blood is clear, but it also ties closely to love and passion. Anger and danger can be inferred as well. The hue is hard to miss and will easily dominate a scheme if you are not careful. When used alongside itself in varying desaturated versions, a striking and rich result

can be achieved. Paired with other colors, it can become a supportive player but must be matched in saturation or lessened intensity to guide the eye as you wish.

Blue—Like green, blue is closely tied to nature. The sky and the sea are blue to most eyes and carry the meanings of royalty and vivid dreaming. Serenity and peace, sadness and melancholy can all be represented in the correct context of color. Depending on how you pair the colors of blue, you can build an air of mystery or confident strength, an airy sense of lightness or stern duty, cold ice or deep thoughtfulness.

Green—As with the leaves and grass and many of the growing things of the world, green is associated with lush places and a sense of natural connection. That natural connection can be twisted and can skew to sickness and rot, but it is still nature, nonetheless. Paired with other hues, green supports and works well with others.

Purple/Violet—Purple is a royal and powerful, rich hue that stands with the brightness of red and the lushness of blue. Perhaps the best of both of those worlds, shades of purple will strike a powerful statement when used—soothing in a way that red struggles to be and loud enough to shame blue in its pretentious reverberations. It works very well against many other hues but is strong in almost any choice. Purple doesn't like to hide.

Orange—Bright and vivid, orange invokes flame and saturated energy. Orange vibrates with power and pride. It is not subtle and speaks to a loud appearance. When desaturated it can meld nicely, however, and it is strong when working in support of colors that are near it on the color wheel—red and yellow particularly. Such combinations increase the inference of flame and fire and are a very specific choice.

Brown—A divination of all previous colors, brown is as diverse as gray. In varying degrees brown can edge closer to any color depending on its composition and usage. Earthy and stalwart, the hues of brown speak of a tie to the ground—not the growing world but the endless power of the rock and mud itself. Brown is primal and simple but strong.

Gray—Gray is a tone, not a hue—but the marriage of black and white is as vast as the combinations and imagination will allow. Neutrality and an absence of color speak volumes. Gray is empty emotionlessness and utilitarian peace, clean and stable.

How long did you sleep? How long were you unconscious after escaping the tunnels that led to this devastated and ruined building? You just aren't certain. The three suns are rising, and the wash of warm pink and yellow light from the sunrise has struck your face and encourages you to pry your eyes open and assess the situation more fully.

In your hand is the Eye of Wonder, a huge red gemstone that glimmers in the morning light with a fiery and almost unnatural glow. When you first heard legends about the gem, you assumed that it was large and beautiful, but holding it now and seeing it here—even in your exhausted state—you are certain that the legends have done it a grave injustice in the description of it.

As you dust yourself off and retrieve your waterskin, you clear a dusty and moss-covered table and unfurl the dry parchment of the map once again. You trace your finger along the path that you have followed thus far and track deeper into the Myth Vale, into the EverWish Glades.

If this massive gem is going to serve to guide you to the true treasure horde, you're going to need to return it to the Sylvan Shrine in the middle of that wild and dangerous place. . . .

Picking through your bag, you realize that most of your gear has been lost or expended in the retrieval of the Eye. You sigh . . . and track your finger back across the map to one of the many campsites that the goblin Thaco Thistle-Britches has marked as regular places for his merchant caravan to offer services and gear.

"Well, well, well . . .

"Look at what the Nether-Beast dragged in.

"When you left a few weeks back, I wasn't so sure that you'd make your way back this direction.

"But it just goes to show that you adventurous types are always full of surprises, and the more that you keep turning up, the more coin that you pull out of the dark and forgotten places of the underground. You're in luck, as that the Eagle Knapsack is still here wasting for some industrious-type hero much like yerself!

"Unfortunately, my wagon had to move farther from the last village due to a mishap with some fireworks that I in no way had anything to do with, and if that donkey told you anything to the contrary, you shouldn't believe it—in fact, you shouldn't really be talking to donkeys at all! They aren't typically any sort of conversationalists and are generally disagreeable and rude.

"It seems that you have just enough coin there to take that pack, so it is yours. Congratulations! Now get outta my shop and put yourself on whatever road leads you to your fate quickest! And don't pet the donkey on your way out. . . ."

The tools and methods of the trade, offered in simple definitions.

When dealing with the complex topic of the science of art, we must remember that I—as your humble guide—am showing you only the very beginning of an academic pursuit that you could spend a lifetime or even two exploring.

In every way, these are guidelines and you, my brave adventurer, must remember that this knowledge is coming through the filter of my twisted and often overworked mind. I am not infallible and am prone to moments of flowery distraction and creative interpretation.

The Path of the Seasoned Sorcerer

As we undertake the first steps of our journey together, let us begin with the foundational skills and techniques that will serve you in all of the projects that you will undertake here in the collected quests within this guidebook and beyond. With these lessons securely understood and implemented, each and every undertaking that you embark upon in the world of hobby painting and crafting will be improved!

QUEST  VII

THACO THISTLE -BRITCHES

Utilizing the goblin merchant Thaco Thistle-Britches, we will explore painting a miniature that is quite different from the Knights of the Myth Vale. Here we have skin tones for the first time in our journey—albeit ones that most humans would find irregular—and a variety of textures and materials to practice upon: leather, cloth, rope, hair, a broom, and—of course—a healthy amount of gold coins and treasure. This is Thaco, after all.

QUEST  VIII

AKORI SOTSONA

The undercoat of material that will ensure adhesion and clarity of the final layers of paint that you will later apply.

QUEST  IX

THE SPITE-FANG KOBOLDS

Base coating is the first stage of painting that will provide the tone, hue, and character that will express our final work.

QUEST X

OA ELVENHEART

A use of washing and careful shading will provide rich contrast and deep, complex areas of darkness to our work in this specific process.

The Eagle Knapsack – B2

The Eagle Knapsack is full to the brim with gear and adventuring tools that, while used, are well maintained and ready to be put into service.

Strangely, the bag is able to carry much more material than its size should allow.

Within it, you find everything that a skilled explorer might need.

✢ **Surface primer**—black

✢ **Acrylic hobby Paints**

- 3 or 4 basic colors

- 1 or 2 metallic paints

- (See the suggested painting resources in section **R1**.)

✢ **Size 1 or 2 brush**

- (The brush should have a sharp point and be bigger than you might think. See the suggested brush resources in section **R2**.)

✢ **Hobby knife** with a few extra blades

✢ **Nail filing stick** with a fine grit

✢ **2 cups, jars**, or **containers** for water

✢ **Palette, paper plate**, or **tile**

✢ **Paper towel, napkins**, or a **cotton rag** (not toilet paper or tissue)

✢ Some **poster tack**

✢ **Empty spool, medicine bottle**, or a bit of **wood**

✢ **Matte varnish**

You've collected the Eagle Knapsack and sit outside of the vardo wagon of the goblin merchant known throughout the land as Thaco Thistle-Britches. Pursuing the material within it, you wonder whether it's going to be enough to get you through the EverWish Forest. Your coin is too thin to purchase much else, and—despite the angry look that the goblin gave the Eye of Wonder—you couldn't possibly trade or sell it.

As you sit there, Thaco appears and tosses a half-eaten apple over his shoulder. The donkey that had been absent-mindedly grazing nearby makes quick work of the treat.

"Look, I've been giving it a little consideration, and given your situation and that gem that you're carrying, I can't in good conscience allow you to find a quick and horrible death in the EverWish Forest.

"Being the upstanding purveyor of fine goods that I am, I see little choice but to guide you through myself. We'll pack up the caravan and take a secret path that only I know, and we'll get you to that elven shrine in no time flat.

"And all that I expect in return is 60 percent of the treasure that we come upon and a favor to be called in at my liking. . . .

"Whaddayasay?" Thaco holds out his small green hand, covered in rings and bangles, for a shake of agreement.

Quest VII
Thaco Thistle-Britches

Putting Color Theory to Work

The colors displayed here will be the basis for Thaco Thistle-Britches's color scheme. He is a goblin merchant and rogue who spends a great deal of time on the road. Earth tones—browns and muted warm tones—will form the majority of the scheme, but the green and pale lavender colors are the focus and used on the face. This combination of subdued tone and brighter, concentrated colors draws our eye to the face. The tertiary use of metallic gold (yellows and oranges) helps our eye to travel after we first land upon the face.

Before we begin with the work of painting our little goblin companion, let's start with a little trick that I have been using for years and that I find makes priming a much easier process, delivering better results and helping to reduce slop and overspray.

You can acquire paint stir sticks at any hardware store for free, but it is also possible to cut and build your own spray stick. A little bit of poster tack will secure your model and allow you to turn the stick in any direction necessary to ensure full and complete coverage.

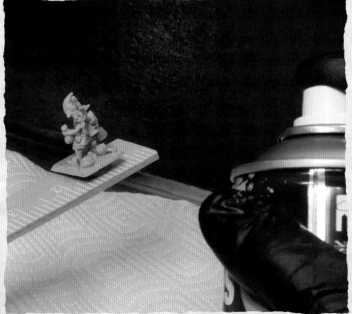

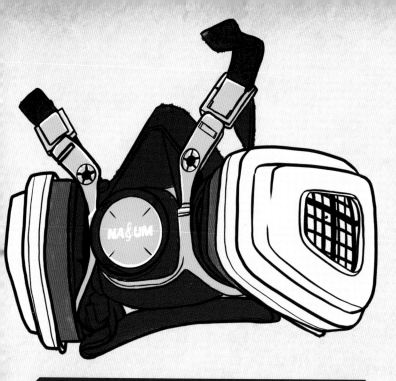

Rattle-can sprays are toxic and can be harmful. Always use a respirator with appropriately maintained filters. (They don't last forever and need to be replaced!) Shake your primer for at least an entire minute and listen to the agitator for the telltale clatter to know that you are sufficiently mixing your material.

The goal here is to hold the stick in one hand while you use your primer rattle can at approximately six inches away from your model. I find that kneading the poster tack before use produces the best results. A school ruler, a strip of thick cardboard, or any long, flat, and lightweight material of about twelve inches in length should do the trick.

In this instance, we are utilizing a basic white undercoat of primer. We'll explore other methods and the results that we can achieve by making different choices, but in this instance, we are choosing white to allow for bright and vivid results. Two or three passes are best. Do not attempt to flood the miniature with primer; it will immediately set you up for failure, and you'll quickly clog and obscure the detail of the model.

Having selected base colors and a few other elements, prepare a palette. Whatever colors you choose, mix a little water into the paint to achieve the smooth, creamy constancy that we've described earlier in our first Quests. Here I'm using a porcelain palette to mix my colors, but you should use what you like. A paper plate, a container lid, an old blister pack from a miniature purchase . . . all are valid options. We'll elaborate and explore other options soon enough.

Starting with the largest areas, how you approach your painting work is a personal thing. I always make a judgment call at the top of a project and determine how sensitive certain areas will be, such as a face, or whether there are large areas of light values. It's easier to repair darker tones than it is to patch a white cloak or redo the large amount of work that you may have spent on a face or other important detail.

Using a painting handle, you can quickly work your way around a model and carefully and neatly fill in the largest areas. I am altering my tan browns and combining lavender to make tones that tie the scheme together but remain warm and earthy. There are three light coats for most of these areas. You can certainly use less, but I have chosen to slightly shift these tones and build subtle shadows and highlights right away. Allowing each layer to dry before moving on, as always, is the way to go to achieve smooth results.

Using a restrained number of colors may seem to restrict your choices, but once you begin mixing your paints, you'll find that you are able to create an impressive and expansive collection of options that allow you to create rich and layered results without distracting the viewer's eye with excessive color sprays.

I'm using the same-size brush, a number 2 with a sharp, well-maintained tip, which allows me to transfer more material to the miniature from the palette without a lot of excessive back and forth, which can cause the paint on your miniature to dry before you can blend the edges of each stoke together. I step down to smaller brushes from time to time, but, in all honesty, if you practice brush control, there is little that you can't accomplish with a weapon this size. Focus, breathe deeply, relax, and feel the calming sea of ability within yourself.

Once we've established a strong and—mostly—complete base coat and have allowed the model to dry fully, we can begin to add some simple and easy definition by either using a premixed wash product or mixing and thinning our own washes, using the base colors that we have chosen and some darker browns and greens to help bolster those shadowed areas. Mixing black directly into your base colors will result in desaturation and dullness. If that is what you seek, it works. Even so, try shades of heavy brown and even some deep reds and see what results you achieve!

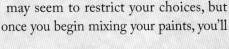

When both the wash and the shade are dry—and you can learn more in **Quest IV** if you are new here—begin to pull the highlights out of the scheme by lightening your core hues. Again, straight white will create flat and chalky results, and I suggest experimenting with mixing pale yellow, light browns, and other off-whites together to create layers that will not sacrifice your vibrancy.

Your miniature is likely on a base of some sort, and while we can explore more in-depth basing in other Quests, I will point out here that the base can be thought of as a frame for your artwork; it is a small window into the world that the miniature lives within. In telling stories, we have a huge opportunity to expand on the viewers' understanding and lead them on further imaginings of the rest of the world that they don't see. Here you can see the pale multitone contrast between warm and cool tones to create a checkerboard style that is subtle and allows the goblin to be the full focus. It supports and doesn't detract.

Adding a clean layer of a darker tone on the rim of a base is the celebratory moment in any project. I save it for last and often sound a war horn loudly and proudly at the end of each. (My neighbors' dogs don't seem to appreciate it as much as I do.) Take a moment and finalize any little mistakes and find your own celebratory habit!

As we undertake this study of our shady little goblinoid ally, I wish to focus on the use of color theory in the scheme that I've chosen for him in this example. If you have a goblin that you'd like to paint using these colors, jump in here and let's work side by side! You'll also find links, at the back of the book in section **R3**, to allow you to order your own Thaco Thistle-Britches, if you'd like to own this model.

Regardless of whether you are interested in painting this grubby little friend, we can use him as a focus to test some of the theory that we've been elaborating on up to this point in your journey. Without further ado, let us bring each of these choices under a magnifying glass and discuss the story that they reveal!

In our color samples at the start of the quest, we can see the three colors that we are focusing on. You may use additional colors and tones, but the core of our concept is currently focused on three. These aren't necessarily easily fit into any single of the basic schemes discussed in our color wheel primer, but the logic is definitely present and being put to good use.

The three hues here are slightly shifted, but if you were to skew them slightly, you'd find that this does hit the triadic scheme.

Green/Orange/Violet—The goblin flesh is muted considerably: the orange is shaded to a variety of warm browns (some edging yellow more than orange), and the violet is more saturated and pushing pink. Still, the logic and guideposts that the triadic foundation creates help us to deviate and create the effect that we are seeking.

Thaco Thistle-Britches is a traveler first and foremost. He's seen the world and is much more of a wanderer than most of the goblins from his clan. His bright skin and hair make it clear that he isn't a dwarf or an elf, and the playful hue of his hair creates an immediate contrast to his skin. Both stand out against the more muted colors of his outfit and hat.

As such, we see from the earthy browns that Thaco is not afraid to get dirty and roll up his sleeves—there is little elegance here. Utility and purpose are the focus of his choices in clothing. Note that the purple appears in the outfit but in a much more muted and desaturated way, to create a harmony without being garish and distracting.

Two days down the valley, away from the mountain to the north and the Kobold Caverns, you begin to believe that your journey is at the risk of becoming monotonous. Perhaps you've been had by the tall tales that Thaco fed you when you spent the last of your coin on the Owl Haversack. Perhaps you're working as a bodyguard and deterrent that happens to be paying their employer. . . .

Potential trickery aside, Thaco Thistle-Britches does seem to know a great deal about the goings-on of the many regions within the Myth Vale. His path to the EverWish Glades is pleasant, and you never would have found it without his aid. Still, there is something in the way that the goblin looks at the horizon that makes you believe that—perhaps—there is merit to the dangers that he has warned of. . . .

The caravan halts near the aged and wholly unsafe-looking bridge that stretches across the deep chasm that plummets down at least 100 feet to a rushing river and rocky shore.

The wagon wheel shatters under the concealed hole that had been dug—deliberately—in the middle of the overgrown pathway. As Thaco examines the trap, he notes the freshness of the turned dirt and leaves that were used to conceal it. One thing is certain: someone wanted you stopped here.

Weapons drawn, you stand at the ready, waiting for the worst possible outcomes. As you seek the hidden foe, you notice Thaco frozen, staring into the heavy tree-lined area that surrounds the road.

He gently motions his head upward, and as you turn, you see her standing above you, twenty lengths into the trees, on a branch, balanced as if standing on firm ground.

A female kitsune with sweeping horns and nine tails that dance with amusement behind her . . .

Quest VIII

Akori Sotsora

Painting Hair and Fur

To continue our journey, let's move to another figure that offers us new challenges and gives us the opportunity to practice techniques that can expand what we've already practiced in earlier Quests.

Akori Sotsora is a kitsune warrior that offers a great deal of fur and texture to work with, along with a pale off-white outfit that lends itself to further work on the subtle progression of tones.

Onward!

We are, once again, utilizing a pure white undercoat to begin the process here. This model offers some exciting opportunities for us to work with a model that has a mixture of flat and textured surfaces. You'll find that while color expresses a great deal of information about our characters, texture is an important addition to our arsenal. You can create texture with your painting and should consider the contrast of different surfaces as you work.

Here you can see that I'm working on a wet palette. If you would like to use one as well, travel to section **R3** in the back of the book to learn more about utilizing these powerfully hydrating paint palettes. I've gathered all of my colors here and have mixed a custom burnt orange for the majority of the fur.

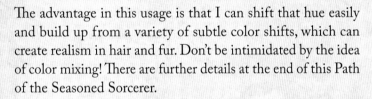

The advantage in this usage is that I can shift that hue easily and build up from a variety of subtle color shifts, which can create realism in hair and fur. Don't be intimidated by the idea of color mixing! There are further details at the end of this Path of the Seasoned Sorcerer.

When working with your primer, much as in the previous Quest, be careful about the distance from which you spray your model. If you are too far away, the spray will dry before hitting your model and will cause a speckled, sandy texture. Be aware of the general temperature and attempt to work outside when possible. Let each layer dry before adding another.

The base coats used here are thin and built up slowly. Use as many layers as you are comfortable with and manage your time as you like. Typically, thin coats built up slowly create much better results, but every color is different, and every painter has very specific thoughts on how best to proceed. As long as you are transferring material onto the model and not obscuring detail, you'll do just fine.

Our kitsune warrior has an orange-brown coloration that transitions into white "socks" and accents. We are painting the areas that we want to bear the majority of the brown-orange in our thin base coat and for the moment leaving be the areas that we want to remain white. Then we are thinning out and darkening our base brown to a wash that will later be thinned

even further into a glaze (**Quest IV** can guide you if you are new here, stranger).

The darker wash is gently worked into the deepest crevices on the model and in the points in which the fur connects to other secretions of the model, such as the Gi, the rest of the outfit, and horns. Once applied, I will wipe the excess off of my brush and blend the wash upward into the base color, taking care not to remove all of the material in the deepest areas. Note that I do not slather the wash across the entire model (a firmly viable technique for speed painting and other efforts; see **Quest XI** for examples that throw such caution from the carriage).

Working the same thinned glaze into the white area of the fur helps us build some definition and transition between the orange-brown fur. Experiment with different dilutions of wash and glaze on the areas of white and focus on the gentle and careful blending of fur to create a realistic result. Once complete, I built an off-white on the Gi and mixed the same brown into white to create a pale tan that I worked up to immediately create highlights and a realistic parchment white.

Mixing a magenta and a red together, I have my accent color that will break up the monochromatic feel and express a little of the playfulness of the character that I am imagining when thinking about this skilled fox warrior and the training that she would have received and the garb that she wears.

Once the shades are fully and completely dry, we can move forward confidently. Remember, a hair dryer can be of great help here but be cautious where you focus the airflow so your washes don't travel where you don't want them. To build up at this point is a matter of refining the mid-tones and highlights. I will often add a small amount of the original base coat to clear up any mistakes made with the darker shades and then mix in lighter hues to render the higher light-struck areas.

As you work, seek to slowly sharpen edges with brighter touches that grow smaller and smaller as you move around the model and become more and more restrained in your applications. To create quicker texture, dry brushing is available, but I challenge you to start here and use some layering and blending before expanding to that tried-and-true technique. Again, **Quest XI** is full of speed-painting methods and sure to scratch that itch. Here, I wish to encourage an understanding of layered applications.

Let's take a moment here at this crossroads and discuss where we've been, so that we can fully understand where we are and where we will be in the future.

The basic applications of paint have been laid out before us, and the seeds of color theory have been planted in fertile ground. We are no longer intimidated by the starting of our work, and we know what we must do to bring us to the point where we currently are. Together we've painted a few miniatures and discussed some of the thinking that supports good hobby habits and a sturdy foundation for future exploration.

In many ways, it is as simple as stalwartly applying paint to our subject and working to maintain the proper consistency and placement. But here is a secret that is, perhaps, not so much of a surprise to those of you who have made as many mistakes in your journeys as I have.

Good painting can improve a badly sculpted model, and bad painting can ruin a well-sculpted model.

That sounds negative, and I suppose that it is. The only bad painting, in truth, is the painting that you don't do at all. Everything is a stepping-stone to greater success, and failing forward is a fine art that I highly recommend to any artist anywhere.

The reason that I bring this to your attention is apparent in this model, our kitsune warrior. There is a lot of texture that is present but more that is implied by the nature of what the creature is. That means that we must move forward in a way that allows us to build texture in areas where it isn't quite strong enough for the effect that we seek to achieve.

To do this, we are going to mix a custom color that we can lighten and darken as we stack the subtly shifted hues in slowly shrinking sections, allowing the previous layer to remain in a thin stripe of paint. With the fur, we can alternate that technique and generate the illusion of depth and variation.

We will begin with this fur, but you will use this skill in many instances of hair and costuming. The idea that texture can be painted translates to leather, metal, cloth, and even skin.

Thaco sputters as he attempts to convince the kitsune warrior to slow her attack. She leaps down in a flash of fur and metal as her spear swirls in the air with deadly accuracy. Wordlessly, she drives the flat end of the spear shaft into Thaco's stomach and throws a bolo at you. Luckily, you are able to drop behind the wagon as the donkey brays loudly and kicks up into the air in protest.

"Whoa! Whoa! Hey now! No need to get violent!" Thaco shouts, ducking again for a swing of the spear. "Why are you doing this?"

A quiet moment. Then you peek under the wagon as you see Thaco on the ground, spear to his throat. The kitsune speaks in a calm and gentle voice: "I know you, thief. You stole the white flour-herb from my village. Those herbs heal our sick, and you paid nothing. Now I think that you will pay more."

You are about to attempt to tackle the kitsune and try to bring some quick resolution to the situation—certainly, Thaco has earned the ire of this warrior—but you know that you would be lost in the forest without him. You could give the kitsune one of the treasure chests that the goblin sleeps under and hope that it covers the village's loss. Before you can do anything, however, a number of feathered spears pierce the ground just a hair's breadth away from the kitsune and goblin. From the undergrowth, a mass of kobold warriors appears and you immediately recognize the markings of the Spite-Fang . . . the same kobolds that you liberated the Eye of Wonder from . . .

Quest IX

THE SPITE-FANG KOBOLDS

PAINTING UNIFIED UNITS AND CREWS

When painting more than a single model, as part of a crew or unit in an even larger army, our utilization of color theory and character design is just as applicable, and we can seek ways to make our scheme uniform and create a strong harmony between individual miniatures.

The colors here on our swatch give us a strong foundation that will be used through multiple models at once, a process known in the miniature hobby world as batch painting. We can create variations to support the idea that each of these models is an individual, but the shared hues will create unity and make a strong appearance on a tabletop or in a display case.

The essence of batch painting is quite straightforward and easy to implement. A painter can best distribute their time by completing a single task across a number of models. After one task is fully accomplished, the second task is completed across the models, and the process continues until you have a finished product.

In this case, rather than use multiple painting handles, corks, or spools, we are working on the miniatures while they remain affixed to the paint stir stick that was used to prime the figures.

If you are working on a large force, separate each of the groups with as many similar models as possible. It will allow you to maintain coherency.

When spraying primer onto a full unit or group of models, the process is much the same, but I recommend that you ensure proper spacing between miniatures. For the kobolds, we are using the black primer. While it lacks the ability to help convey vibrancy, it is perfect for characters with a darker, shadowed feel. If armor and other metal elements are predominate, a black undercoat will be extremely helpful.

Working on each model in this method is efficient and allows you to assess each stage of the process and to refine layers in groups before moving forward and adding additional layers. By the time that you are finished with the last model, the first model should have the most recent coat dry and will be ready to be advanced further.

Whether you are painting a unit, a crew, an entire army, or just a handful of creatures for your weekly tabletop role-playing adventure, batch painting, when correctly implemented, not only can speed your efforts but also can improve the cohesion and visual interest of the group as a whole.

In determining the colors that you wish to use, rather than simply considering the background and story of a single individual, put some thought into the collective force. Why are these beings working together? Are they part of a uniformed patrol?

Have they been hired by a wizard to guard a treasure? Are they a ragtag band of heroes gathered to deliver a dangerous treasure somewhere? How long have they traveled together? These sorts of questions can help guide you to answers that will determine the schemes that you will use to tell these stories.

If you are interested in exploring these sorts of questions more fully, you can find the character inquiry questionnaires in **C1** deeper in this manual.

In this particular instance, the information that we are working from has been determined by the story that we have been inhabiting as we travel through the Myth Vale in the search of the altar of the elven people in the EverWish Forest.

These kobolds work as a long line of protectors of the grave of an ancient dragon that once held a great horde in the mountain range known to the villagers of Thent as the Kobold Caverns. They live in a mountainous area, they are all related to one another, and they typically remain in dark places.

To communicate this, we will use warm earth tones to denote a sense of connection to the crags of their homeland. As an accent, we will use subtle touches of red to signal the color of the dead dragon that they once served, and their scales will all be shades of blue and purple. The choice of hue will create a nice balance between the other colors and will make for a perfect and immediate signifier that these creatures are most likely from the same clutch of kobolds.

The colors that have been chosen are laid out on the palette and are being slightly shifted toward a blue tone here. This creates a realistic variation in the group, but as we are using the majority of the same base-cast purple, all members of the entire unit seem easily related to each other without being flat and monotonous.

When moving onto the armor and leather, the garb and gear, your key color choices can also be slightly altered as you move among the models, but be sure not to bog yourself down with custom mixing at this stage. Remember that the goal here is to focus our process and produce quick results over a larger number of models. Try to put a solid set of paint coats on each of the sections and shift back to the first.

As you can see, the steps do not deviate greatly in the execution of the process. Shades and highlights can be as lavish or as simple as you see fit. Each step that you add, however, will add to the time that you are investing into the entire force. Be sure to establish clear goals and don't complicate your efforts beyond the allowances of time that you have determined are appropriate for the project.

Using inks can greatly expand your glazing and washes; they do not behave the same as acrylic paint and should be carefully handled. You can achieve impressive aging and rust colorations through the careful application of ink in selected areas. I recommend sealing them with a matte sealer before moving forward and—for simplicity at this point—using exclusively water-based products.

Tightening the details can become consuming but be sure to take moments to stretch and take breaks, rest your eyes and hands, and allow your mind to clear itself before returning—then assess your work. Reviewing a batch with fresh eyes and judging the pieces based on how they look is tougher at a short distance and will give you a clear view of what you need to finish the group to your wishes.

If you are content with the work that you've accomplished up to this point, you can separate the miniatures from their groups and pick out the tiny last details that will create some small amount of individuality and give each some unique touches. While fully optional, a little attention spent on each of the models outside of the batch work can create just enough visual interest and realism.

our sword in your hand, you swing into the fierce kobold. As the blue-scaled little reptile stabs at you, you see its beady yellow eyes sizing you up. Two others quickly join the first, and the three begin to herd you backward with their crude but effective weapons.

Back-to-back with the kitsune and Thaco Thistle-Britches, it would seem that the conflict between the strange fox person and the goblin has come to an abrupt end.

"I don't suppose that either of you has any idea on how best to escape thirty angry kobolds?"

As you and your newfound companions fight desperately forward, an impressive number of kobolds have been pushed back and—for a moment—it feels as though the three of you might be able to flee into the forest.

As the kitsune—who has in a quick shout identified themselves as Akori—leaps across the overgrown roadway, a large, thuggish kobold emerges to block the passage.

In the moment, you realize that surrender may be the only option.

Then, in a hail of arrows, the kobolds break and flee back the way that they came. Looking to the ground, you see a perfectly crafted white arrow shaft with a thick white feathered quill and a faintly carved series of vines and leaves.

Identical arrows pierce the ground in a perfect circle around you, Thaco, and Akori.

And, as if things weren't already bad, now you've brought the attention of the elves. . . .

Quest

Oa Elvenheart

Replicating Skin Tones

In this Quest we will be undertaking the **rendering of human skin tones**. In understanding how to paint a variety of skin tones, we are able to tell more expansive and interesting stories. As we can tell from our modern real world, people come in a beautiful diversity of shapes, colors, and sizes. Our fantasy worlds are made richer when they reflect a variety of life. So let's get to work!

With our elven sword mage, Oa Elvenheart, we will begin with a darker skin tone and a soft blue tunic; however, I will guide you, dear friend, through some of the variations available and how best to mix and handle a variety of skin tones.

I have chosen to work off of the wet palette in this Quest, but feel free to utilize whatever surface that you are most comfortable with. If you are ready to explore the world of wet palettes—and to perhaps determine whether they are the correct tool for your usage—make your way to later sections to learn about all of the requirements, preparations, and materials that you'll need to meet to get started.

For our example here, I've mixed an original base tone using a blend of blue, magenta, yellow, and white. This blend creates a rich, warm brown, but if you alternate the amounts of these colors, you can make a wide variety of flesh tones.

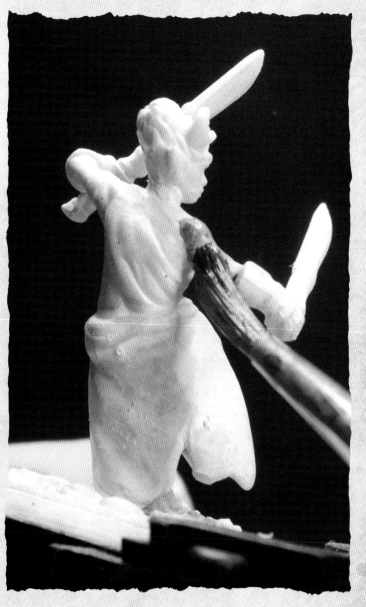

Many companies offer a plethora of premixed paint colors for you to use immediately in creating a bounty of skin tones, but never feel obligated to rely entirely on material that you feel is a compromise just in order to avoid mixing paint.

Before we lay down the first thin applications of our chosen base skin tone, we should ensure that we have a smooth and clear prime coat off of which to build. White is a strong choice, but feel free to experiment if you are looking to create darker, more shadowed, grim results. Here we are working in white to promote a vibrant and powerful appearance of both tone and hue.

In most instances, I will lay in the skin tones first and build outward. While we are painting a tunic in white—which can be intimidating—if we make any mistakes at this stage, we can touch it up before moving forward. Again, painting order and other such decisions are left to your personal preference and can shift wildly between painting sessions.

The rich skin tone of this elven warrior is a perfect contrast to the flowing pale robes that they are wearing. Other contrast can be found in the metals of the swords and the circlet, the bracers, and the sandals. By marking out the major sections of a model and carefully picking out the details in our chosen base coat colors, we are able to quickly get a sense of the balance between our choices.

Shades and highlights, as explained in **Quests IV** and **V**, can alter the base color significantly once laid in place, and you should consider where you want the final tones and hues to end up once you are finished.

There is a wide and wonderful variety of skin tones available to us to use as reference, and maintaining a small library of images—electronic or otherwise—can make a world of difference in the rendering of the myriad flesh tones within the world. Add to that the possibility of more fantastical flesh tones, such as electric blue or green, and the method with which we render skin becomes crucial across the color wheel.

It is best to understand how to create tone outside of hue, so that you can replicate believable skin regardless of the color choices that you have made. Think about the way that light interacts with skin: it is translucent, and a variety of colors appear in both pale and dark skin tones. The approaches with which you might tackle these two extremes are somewhat different, but many of the underlining principles are the same.

Skin is best applied in very thin coats, so water down your paints to a ratio that provides you with very delicate applications, working up from a very thin base coat that might require three coats to many filters of another hue in the form of glazes.

As for our miniature here, first, I am gently feathering the glazes of purple and blush-brown into the recesses, using them both—and a variety of mixtures in between—to create the warm layers that build contrast and depth. I am careful to allow each layer to fully dry before applying another.

Using a heavily diluted basic black paint, mixed 50/50 with a warm dark brown and thinned considerably, I begin creating additional definition and separation of the flesh from the other areas of the model. Using a dark brown or gray, alone, will suffice here as well, but I find that a pure black and a mixture of deep brown creates the strong contrast and visual division that I—personally—prefer. Use the very tip of your brush, stepping down to a smaller brush if needed, and trace along the recesses of the varied elements of the model. The process is called black lining by some.

Using a more traditionally diluted paint, in this example, I have prepared a number of highlights that are built from the original base color. Adding more beige and chestnut brown in gradual amounts with just a touch of blue, I am working to create paler layers and shades that we can blend into the highest points on the flesh—always seeking to replicate light upon the flesh tone shown here. Remember to always consider your fictional light source and paint accordingly.

In creating highlights and when blending, especially when dealing with skin tones, the placement of paint can become somewhat daunting. Please, do not fear this process. Simply take each step slowly. Remember your imagined light source and draw an imaginary line in your mind from the light source(s) that strike the model in your fantasy world; use the points that are closest to that source to determine the brightest areas. Note the quality of the light and keep shadows in the recesses with a gradual fade to your highlights. Soften your transitions as much as you like through blending.

Once the basic tones are dry, we will create a series of thin glazes that we can use to slowly shade and blend shadows into the recesses of the model. Refer to **Quests III** and **IV**, if necessary, to review the ratios and basics of mixing and thinning your paints. Glazes are extremely effective in painting skin tone, as the subtle and careful layers that can be gradually accumulated create marvelous depth that allows the previous layers to show through, making the model feel alive through the varied shifts in skin tone

To smooth out all of your work and assist the transitions between the layers that you've applied, return to your glazes and slowly apply thin filtering layers, allowing each to dry before moving on. Here, I tend to return to a hue that is close to the first base coat—what should now be our mid-tone. You can use redder versions of your original flesh color to build blush on the cheeks, nose, lips, and other areas with increased blood flow. In this example, purples and greens served me well in applying dramatic shade and lively variation in the skin.

The Adventurer's Guild
Exploring the Unknown

In review of our journey thus far, we have studied the base skills of the arts and crafts that our hobby requires, and we've enacted the use of these skills in the completion of a few Quests that have challenged us to put those skills to use and to begin the journey that will lead us into advanced studies and exercises.

Yet in all of this we have continued to discuss the importance of storytelling in the process, and while technical understanding is important, much of the knowledge that I have to impart upon you is more ephemeral than the standard methods and tried-and-true practices that have been developed over the ages.

Knowing how to paint your miniatures is different from knowing how to tell stories through your miniatures. Technique will allow you to accomplish your goals, but those goals must be determined beforehand and come from within you!

Now, perhaps you are perfectly content to follow along with the box art of a set of miniatures—to dutifully replicate the figures that are displayed on the packaging. More power to you.

There is a great amount to be learned through replication, and I have done so in the past.

But my argument to those of you who seek something more challenging is that the rewards of gathering your personal experience and style and applying both to the subjects you choose is the difference between paint by numbers and a creating art on a blank canvas.

But how do you make the choices that allow you to create unique and original results? It can feel as if you are standing on the edge of a cliff. That feeling of exposure—looking out into an unknown destination—it can be a wonderful thing; while it can also be intimidating, it can also provide great freedom.

Embrace it and I will do my best to give you some of the tools that may help you along the way. If you are ever stuck, feel free to use the charts and story prompts that I've supplied you with here to help to determine some parts of the story that might guide your imagination forward as you select colors and create new worlds.

Holding the Eye of Wonder in front of you, the fading sunlight appears speckled through the treetops and thick branches of lush green Fallowheart trees, and the red gem dances and glows as if lit from within by some magical, unseen light. The elves—the very picture of composure, cold, emotionless control, and training—share a number of subtle glances among themselves, as close to a wild reaction as could be expected from ancient and highly skilled masters of sword and spell.

"We seek to return the Eye of Wonder to the ancient shrine in the ruins at the heart of this glade. We mean no offense and will leave when our work is complete."

The same elven woman, clearly the leader of this force of warriors, holds her hand up, palm to the sky.

"Consider your quest at its end. Give me the Eye and I will see it to its home. In return, we shall grant you safe passage out of our lands."

You swallow hard, knowing that you won't be able to do that. Your quest is to learn the path to the lost treasure that will be revealed when the gem is properly seated in the altar. You must be the one to guide it home.

"If only I could accept your offer, but my companions and I are honor bound by ancient rites to see the task done."

Both Akori and Thaco shoot you looks of surprise and perhaps anger. In for a penny, in for a pound. In your estimation, you need help, and if the elves believed you all to be honor bound together, it would be hard for them to kill each other. For the moment, at least . . .

With this parchment, you can randomize your choices and roll a pair of ten-sided dice (2 D10) to create a direction that may help to spur you forward with the barrier of indecision removed. Conversely, if you are not so hampered, perhaps you are seeking a challenge that will test your skills and force you to work within the confines of colors and tones that you do not naturally gravitate toward.

	1	2	3	4	5	6	7	8	9	0
1	R	B	Y	G	O	P	Br	Gr	Bk	W
2	B	Y	G	O	P	Br	Gr	Bk	W	R
3	Y	G	O	P	Br	Gr	Bk	W	R	B
4	G	O	P	Br	Gr	Bk	W	R	B	Y
5	O	P	Br	Gr	Bk	W	R	B	Y	G
6	P	Br	Gr	Bk	W	R	B	Y	G	O
7	Br	Gr	Bk	W	R	B	Y	G	O	P
8	Gr	Bk	W	R	B	Y	G	O	P	Br
9	Bk	W	R	B	Y	G	O	P	Br	Gr
0	W	R	B	Y	G	O	P	Br	Gr	Bk

R - Red   B - Blue   Y - Yellow   G - Green   O - Orange   P - Purple   Br - Brown   Gr - Gray   Bk - Black

There is no failure that won't, in some way, instruct you on your future successes. Embrace the unknown and explore without fear.

Should you find yourself fully without direction and seeking some sort of basic starting point for your miniature work, why not leave your key color selection to the Hands of Fate?

As we will explore in greater detail, color has a language that speaks to us on a primal level. It can be tracked all the way back to our earliest artistic interpretations and helps to express our relationship with the world around us. The verdant glow of a lively green creates a much different subconscious reaction than the sharp, bright, angry blaze of a pure red.

We can contrast and subvert those instinctual reactions, but to understand them and to practice a number of combinations and usages will be of great value to us in the future.

Roll the dice and determine your color, or two, or three. How brave are you?

Understanding that all artistic storytelling is a path of exploration and discovery, we must be prepared to ask many questions of ourselves as we make decisions that define the story that we wish to tell, the character that we wish to render, and the world that we are seeking to create a window into.

But what are the right questions to ask?

When you pick up a miniature that you wish to paint, what is the first thought that you have?

Traveling on foot, having left Thaco's wagon securely locked up on the side of the road, the party trudges through the thick, overgrown glade. While he was willing to leave the wagon behind, the goblin refuses to travel into the forest of the elves without his donkey and is now slowly guiding the stubborn beast a short distance behind the rest of the outsiders.

Moving quickly among the branches above, the elven guards continue to watch over and guide you. They are clearly making their presence known, and whether it is to facilitate your travel through these endlessly confusing woods or as a show of force that is meant to keep you in line. . . .

You know that if they determine that your intentions are less than good, you may not need to worry about the pathway back to the road.

What are the most striking details? Where is your eye naturally drawn? What sorts of materials are incorporated into the garb and equipment of the character?

These studies are determined, first, by the goals that you have for your painting work.

What is the model to be used for?

Is this a hero that will lead a unit of warriors during a tabletop war game, or is this just one of fifty troops that you must complete before your army can be made tournament ready?

Or is this your character for a role-playing adventure that you wish to provide with an appropriate and personalized pawn? Have you forsworn the use of bottle caps and the remains of your childhood board game collections? Are you seeking to replicate the details that define your hero in the glory of 28-mm artistry?

Gathering the information that will best help you to select the schemes and styles that you will implement in your painting may begin with understanding of how much time you have to expend and what the final goal is for your work, but the heart and soul of our work is in the story that we wish to tell. For that we will begin to examine things from a less practical and more magical eye.

Here we ask your imagination to run wild.

Who is the model that you have chosen to paint? What is their life like? Are they wealthy or poor? Are they old or young? Are they servants to a local liege, or are they simple farm folk who have taken up arms to seek a world of adventure?

Many such questions are easy for models that represent characters from tabletop role-playing games, but the exploration of how your answers to these questions translate into color can be a little more difficult.

If you are painting for a war game or a mass of models for a display, take some time to explore the source material and mine any information that may lead you to a discovery that could be used to help refine your choices and bring your story to life. If you are leaning on your own creativity, think about those whom such groups may serve. What are the colors of a nation's flag? What is the environment that the force lives within? What are the values that they fight for?

Once you start to determine these elements, the direction of your color choices will be much easier.

But what does each of the colors within the spectrum represent in those instinctive reactions that we discussed earlier in these past Quests?

To the right, you'll find a brief explanation; you can also reference the color wheel located before **Quest VII** to visually explore some simplified definitions. And, as we've already mentioned, these are guidelines, and the generally accepted thoughts regarding the relation of each emotion and representation of color can be subverted and reinvented based on both the subject perspective of the viewer and the relations to the form in which it is used.

Rather than attempting to force something to mean only one thing, we can follow along the means of thought that encourage us to accept that perspective and reality are as diverse as the division of people able to engage it.

Simply put, we can say that something is filled with meaning but that meaning is as shifting as the sand and can only be held as potential rather than immutable.

Passing a large fallen Weirwood of aged gray bark, covered in thick blankets of green and blue moss, a thick cloud of floating pollen and motes of fallow seed fills the air like suspended tiny stars locked in the dark of the grove. The night is bright; the moons in the sky are burning with the summer glow as they loom close and big in the sky at this time of the annual cycle.

If your lives weren't on the line, you might become easily lost in the beauty of the place. Akori has been quietly asking you questions, and you have done your best to explain yourself and your quest. At the moment, it would seem that you are now responsible for paying the debt that Thaco owes the kitsune thrice-fold and that the bright-eyed fox person would be traveling with you until such time as the debt is repaid.

The elves believe that an honor-bound oath has been spoken, and now Akori is holding you to it.

Somewhere behind you, Thaco continues to spit curses as he and the donkey stumble in the darkness.

The silence then hits you like a war hammer to the gut as the elves immediately halt themselves and stand in the trees looking toward an open swath of thick green grass and a gentle sloping mound with a circle of jagged stone: the altar of the sylvan spirits.

You stand before an ancient and forgotten ruin of the elven people . . . the seat of the Eye of Wonder. . . .

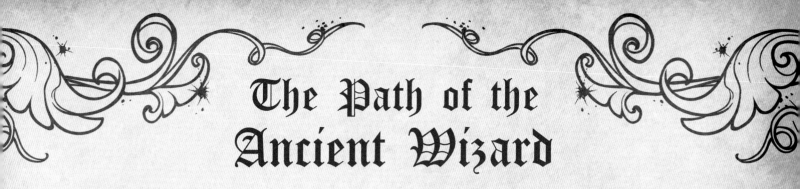

The Path of the Ancient Wizard

As we undertake the first steps of our journey together, let us begin with the foundational skills and techniques that will serve you in all of the projects that you will undertake here in the collected Quests within this guidebook—and beyond. With these lessons securely understood and implemented, each and every undertaking that you embark upon in the world of hobby painting and crafting will be improved!

QUEST

THE ENDLESS HORDES

In painting a large number of miniatures at once, efficient and effective techniques become the key to success in your hobby goals. In this Quest, we will explore methods of speed painting to quickly make entire armies and slews of models ready for your game table.

QUEST

THE DRAGON

Our final Quest centers around the unique challenges and the excitement of painting larger models and monsters using a selection of the techniques that we've acquired in our journeys together. We'll focus on airbrushing techniques and finish with some advanced glazing and painting.

QUEST

BASING YOUR MINIATURES

Once you have lavished a miniature with a careful paint job, there is an opportunity to heighten the realism and to tell more of the story in the application of scenic basing. Here, we will look at a variety of options and methods to put your subject on a base worthy of admiration.

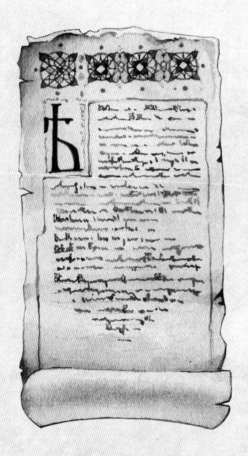

The Owl Haversack - B3

The Owl Haversack is heavy and dense with advanced dungeoneering equipment that boggles the mind and challenges your understanding of the craft. This bag must have once been carried by an eccentric mage or widely traveled scholar. Brass and clockwork mechanisms greet you, and rolls of parchment that contain copious amounts of instructions on their use are held within the slick leather pack.

It smells of strange smoke and incense and has a few specks of blood staining its sides. . . .

This is the advanced equipment of an adventurer who is at the end of their journey.

✢ **Everything from the Raven Rucksack and Eagle Knapsack**

✢ **A selection of inks**

- 3 or 4 basic colors

- (See the suggested painting resources in section **R1**.)

✢ An additional **size 2 brush**

- (The brush should have a sharp point and be bigger than you might think. See the suggested brush resources in section **R2**.)

✢ A **cheap synthetic brush** that will be ruined

✢ **Nail Filing stick** with a fine grit

✢ An airbrush and compressor (see section **R3**), optional

✢ **Airbrush thinner** and a few **cups**

✢ **Black foam core**

✢ Some form of low-moisture **craft glue**

✢ **Milliput** or **Green Stuff**

✢ A **metal straight edge** or **ruler**

✢ **Wood glue**

✢ **Clean dirt** and/or **sand**

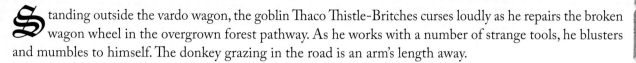

Standing outside the vardo wagon, the goblin Thaco Thistle-Britches curses loudly as he repairs the broken wagon wheel in the overgrown forest pathway. As he works with a number of strange tools, he blusters and mumbles to himself. The donkey grazing in the road is an arm's length away.

"I knew that this was going to end up being a raw deal for ol' Thaco. It's the look of you. All spit and fire, heroism and impatience. You didn't have to leave the Eye of Wonder behind; those elves hadn't seen it in a hundred, hundred cycles and didn't lift a finger to put it back on that crusty altar."

His hammer is tapping frantically at a peg as the wheel nears completion. *"So what now—that red beam of light that leapt across the grove and struck that giant rock has shown you the way to a great treasure?"*

You have been slowly working on a bit of dried fruit leather as Akori meditates on the roof of the wagon. *"Actually, yes. I struck an old elven sigil that means 'hearth.'"*

The goblin sputters, *"OHHHHHHHH! Hearth, is it? Well, that clears it up neatly, don't it? Now we just need to search every hearth in the kingdom for a hidden treasure. . . . Should only take a thousand cycles."*

You can't help but smile. *"No . . . not so difficult as that. The hearth that sigil is referring to is the Hearthfire Mountain. It's telling us where the treasure is hidden and how to find it. We just need to find a way to deal with the dragon."*

Thaco's hammer drops to the ground. *"The what?"*

You have traveled far, hero, to stand at the threshold of these last pathways. I believe that as you continue your journey well beyond the instruction and wit and whimsy held within these pages, your growth will meet many crossroads that reflect the one before you now.

Miniature painting and hobby crafting rarely take you in a straight line, and your discoveries and explorations will often deviate in ways that surprise you. Even now, in my advancing years, I find curiosities and rediscover forgotten treasures. At some points you may find that you are walking in circles and not making the progress that you expected; still, you will be stronger in your craft for it.

If I am able to impart only a single piece of wisdom here, then—please—take this:

Celebrate your failures and learn from them. Judge yourself by the measurement of yourself yesterday and not against others whose days and struggles are unknown to you.

In that spirit, what have we accomplished to this point? As we discussed in the Adventurer's Guild section, we have learned some techniques and studied the foundations of story in our craft and how to infuse our work with rich thought and intention.

Honing the basics and stepping into the more advanced techniques that will aid us in the future—and tilling the earth of storytelling to plant the seeds of greater successes in our work—is well and good, but the final three quests are going to offer gateways to further study as we must, soon enough, part ways for now.

In the **Endless Hordes**, your skills will be tested and put to the flames of the greatest foe of any miniature painter: a sea of unpainted figures and not enough time to complete them! Speed painting is a skill that, much like batch painting, requires you to plan carefully and to budget yourself and your time even more severely. I will arm you with a series of exercises that ask you to time yourself and make improvements that do not prevent the completion of well-painted work!

Finally, we will face a beast that offers us the opportunity to practice advanced techniques and **examine the airbrush**, whether it is a tool worthy of your personal arsenal, and how best to grapple with large projects. Dragons are one of the most rewarding, challenging, and entertaining subjects in the realms of fantasy, and this model will become a centerpiece in your collection!

The Hand of Fate - Schemata Scatter

Roll 1 D20 (one twenty-sided die) to determine the scheme that you will use for your figures

#	Description	Key Tone	Supporting Hues/Tints	Details
1	Lawful Good - Guardians and protectors known for a purported purity and justice.	warm white	yellow and blue (H)	brown and tan
2	Lawful Neutral - Law and order above all things. The realms are bound in law, and it must be obeyed.	deep blue	gray and black (H)	white and tan
3	Lawful Evil - To rule above all without challenge or question, to be the authority that is followed.	indigo	black and purple (H)	crimson and silver
4	Neutral Good - Like the winds of the sky and the whim of the sea, nature sets all right.	tan	white and brown (H)	gray and yellow
5	True Neutral - All things are as they should be, and we exist to but observe the movement of the planes.	gray	white and black (T)	supporting tones
6	Neutral Evil – Power is free to those that take it.	dark brown	black and gray (T)	tan
7	Chaotic Good - Bending the rules and breaking tradition but always following their heart.	red-orange	pale blue and mint green (T)	brown and tan
8	Chaotic Neutral - Hello. How are you? Did you drop your magic hamster? I have a spare if you need one.	orange	blue-green and violet (T)	red and yellow
9	Chaotic Evil - Power unfettered; nothing will stop or slow the progress of the strong and dominant.	crimson	black and violet (T)	gray and dark brown
10	Forest Child - The touch of the wild places of the world is clear, and the seasons shift and reflect mood and garb.	green	brown and yellow (T)	yellow and tan
11	Mountain Guard - Stone and steel, the cold, unforgiving reaches of the high places and harsh survival.	gray	blue-violet and brown (T)	black and white
12	Seaward Wanderer - The endless seas churn and shift and carry you to the horizon; peace and chaos are joined.	blue-green	blue and blue-violet (T)	gray and white
13	Swamp Dweller - Rotted and fetid pools of thick and dark mystery, the secrets of nature turned to death.	black	brown and gray (T)	yellow-green
14	Plains Hunter - To stalk and stride in the open places and fields of sun-drenched grass and grain.	tan	yellow and white (H)	brown
15	Arcane Caster - Bending reality to the will of the ancient arts of magick; scholar and outsider.	blue-violet	blue and gray (T)	black and white
16	Sneak Thief - The shadows call, and the answer is to take that which can be; no honor here but much skill.	charcoal	black and blue-violet (H)	gray
17	Sworn Sword - Negotiating with steel and grit, warriors of note and legend never hesitate to heed the call.	blue	silver and tan (H)	brown and white
18	Healing Hand - Guided by faith and a willingness to cure and heal, to stop the darkness that creeps close.	cool white	pale yellow and brown (H)	red-violet and yellow-orange
19	Traveling Troubadour - Song and tale for a coin; the road beneath boots and the freedom to roam.	red	violet and orange (H)	blue-green and red-violet
20	The Royal Treatment - All hail the liege of the land, the crown bearer and protector of the realm.	purple	gold and blue (H)	black and tan

Quest XI

The Endless Hordes

Speed Painting

In this Quest, we will be utilizing the skills that we have practiced but will do so with a clear plan of action that allows us to move very quickly in our work on a large number of models. We will set goals and plan accordingly as we define what is crucial and what can be left undone in our painting.

Give yourself a realistic goal for the entire project. This is determined by how many models you are attempting to finish and what your desired results are. Be realistic and don't become too precious when determining what steps you will undertake and what you will leave to the side.

In this Quest, I am using an airbrush to create a simple zenithal highlight. To do this, I begin with a black undercoat and then spray a gray and white layer on a single top-ward area, leaving the black in the shadows and creating an instantaneous under-painting that helps define high contrasts and lighting.

Mixing for the airbrush is the most crucial step when working with this tool. Airbrushes clog quite easily, but the effects and speed that you can harness in their use are well worth the effort and difficulty. Thinning paints is always important, but in the use of the airbrush, it is doubly critical.

In selecting the color palette that I will be using on these models, I have chosen a lot of neutral earth tones and will be using a great deal of weathering and washing to accentuate the details and create visual interest.

A selection of disposable stir sticks is invaluable in this process alongside small, shallow plastic cups. While mixing our paint for use in an airbrush, it becomes an easy thing to waste material or to not properly stir and disperse the material in the thinner.

Using small amounts of poster tack, here you can see that I have created some rough and quick masking to block the areas of the model that I do not want to paint with the airbrush.

Airbrushes and Oil Washes

As mentioned before in earlier Quests, an airbrush can be an amazing tool and create wonderful effects easily and quickly, but the trade-offs in equipment costs and maintenance are not to be disregarded.

This all said, once you are ready to cross that threshold—as expensive and complex as the process may be—you will be rewarded with the ability to produce amazingly smooth transitions, thin applications, and some of the quickest and most professional-looking results possible with any tool. In this usage, it isn't so much the artistry of the airbrush that makes it effective here but rather the science.

Oil washing is also a hugely effective technique that can help to instantly improve your artistic efforts and increase the quality of and speed with which you paint. However, oil paint must be cleaned using white mineral spirits and should be used with care. The material itself does not dry quickly, taking hours and hours to fully set—sometimes days. You'll need to master the use of spray varnishes before you use oils extensively, and you won't want to use your good brushes, as the oil and mineral spirits quickly ruin any brush that you might utilize.

To understand the use and mechanics of the airbrush, you can journey to the final Quests of this book, where I explain the most basic functions and usages of the tool. Here, I am laying down the primed zenithal coats and some of my key hues, the bone and some gray, on the cloth and weapons.

Trigger control and air pressure management are crucial in properly utilizing your airbrush. Keeping the PSI—or air pressure measurement—low enough to allow you control but high enough to spray and atomize the paint is a skill that is acquired with practice. Each paint is going to require different PSI adjustments; 60–90 PSI is a safe starting point.

Here I am using more poster tack and a tool to manipulate it into place so that I can spray other areas on the model but not ruin the work that I have already done. This, of course, means that your previous coats of paint should be fully dried before proceeding.

This process can save a hobbyist a great deal of time and help accelerate overall painting output. That said, there is always a price. Cleaning and maintaining the tools, the price of the necessary tools and materials, and the ease of use—including the matter of safety and ventilation—are all considerations.

Working slowly and carefully, I am applying the second airbrush color on the model and carefully painting the deep recesses while gradually preparing those spaces for other applications. The lighter bone colors are safe and sound under our protective shield of blue poster tack. Other materials may be used in masking, including bits of low-stick tape, a bit of cardstock, or even your thumb.

After the second paint tone is dry, I carefully remove the poster tack and mixture of mineral spirits and oil paint to perform a series of weathering washes that will give our speed-painted skeleton some unbelievable depth and interest with very little effort.

Without being too persnickety about the process, lay on a generous wet coat of the oil wash and ensure that the deepest recesses are fully coated. This will darken the entire model and may create some small amount of concern when you first place it. Trust me—you aren't ruining your work! We will be removing a large amount of the accumulated material in the next steps.

The materials here are easily accessible but do require some additional considerations when being brought into your painting arsenal. Oil paint is a different beast from acrylic paint and must be handled with care. Mixing mineral spirits with oil paint, I am seeking to create a thin, tinted material that isn't too thick. It is okay to leave a blob of paint in the mineral spirits while you work with the watery oil wash that collects around it.

After applying the black oil wash, I give the umber oil wash a quick stir and drop it down on the skeleton bone and areas where rust and grim might accumulate. The two washes may blend together in some areas, but this can be used to your advantage: the mingling of tones can produce interesting and realistic transitions.

After allowing the oil wash to dry to the touch—oil paint can take an exceptionally long time to thoroughly dry—I use a densely packed, pointed cotton swab dipped in mineral spirits and slowly begin removing the majority of the dried oil on the top layers of texture on the skeleton.

This process can be accomplished with a synthetic brush as well, and is the basis for the oil-washing technique. Oil paint is quite easily activated with just a bit of mineral spirits at any point in the process. It dries to the touch in a few hours but will require more time to fully cure. This makes it—while somewhat more complicated to work with—very useful in blending and creating beautiful transitions on your piece.

With the oil wash completed, we are ready to allow it to fully dry and then to continue on using the layering and shading techniques that we've learned in our earlier Quests. Painting on top of oil washes is much the same as any other work, but I often use a matte varnish spray to help secure all of the work up to this point. It also reduces the glossy sheen that oil paint can produce.

As this model is being treated as a single member of a very large unit used in war gaming, the time spent on the details of the model should be proportionate to the use of that model. I'll go into this in more detail soon, but as we saw in **Quest IX**, batch painting and other tricks of the trade can help us speed up our work considerably. This model is meant to be completed quickly—get to it!

The exact time that you spend on your speed painting is up to you—and wholly relative to your skill level and desired outcome. I won't make any statements about what is considered a good speed-painting time frame, as it is up to you to determine it for yourself. My advice, however, is that you time yourself and work to achieve a time that you find challenging but not stressful. This model was not lavished with much attention at all, and I am still pleased with it.

Speed Painting Explained and Explored

Clearly accepting the use of the model will help you to budget an appropriate amount of effort based on your desired results. Your role-play hero may well be worth ten hours of work, but is the lone trooper who will stand among fifty of their siblings on the game table?

The answers must come from you and you alone. I will, however, caution you not to fall into the trap that many before you have tumbled into headfirst. Unless you seek to be a competition display painter and have little concern about the utility of your miniatures, do not allow yourself to mire yourself in a fruitless use of your talent and time in trying to make each and every model that you undertake in perfect detail with lavish amounts of attention.

The right amount of time to spend on each can be determined through some forethought and a little internal audit regarding your goals as a painter and how much time you have available.

Time Available Divided by Models to Complete Equals Painting Time for a Single Model:

(TA/M = TSM)

Fighting forward, Akori leaps across the crumbling stone bridge and kicks the accursed skeleton across the jaw, sending the armored nightmare tumbling into the rushing dark river below, to be lost in the twisting waters. The nine-tailed fox kin look back at their companions and the horde of walking dead that crowds both sides of the river and—increasingly—the bridge itself.

Thaco Thistle-Britches and his wagon sit firmly in the middle of the ancient bridge, his donkey braying loudly as the skeletons press in closer and closer. He shuffles through a number of crates and tosses a wild array of sundry items into the air as he desperately seeks to locate something to help the adventuring party move forward. A cheese grater, a bedroll, and a full string of garlic are all tossed off of the roof of the vehicle as you—sword drawn—stand at the ready, seeking a way out of fighting an entire skeletal army.

It certainly isn't looking good—with the pathway set before you and your companions, the EverWish Forest behind you, and the secrets of the elven glade revealed, unimaginable treasure awaits you . . . assuming that you don't become another of these lifeless warriors before the end of the night.

These risen dead have given you no respite, and they are countless, surrounding you in their rusted and decaying armor. Whatever battleground these warriors pulled themselves up from, their former war is long forgotten, and friend and foe now move with singular purpose: destroy the living. It would almost be poetic if it wasn't quite so deadly.

Thaco shouts from the top, *"Found it!"* With the spark of a tinder twig and a bright blaze, a single white candle is lit. Its light causes the skeleton warriors to push back from the glow that it emits. *"What? Why does everyone seem so surprised that I have something useful?"*

The caravan lurches forward down the dark, moonlit cobblestone road. The candle burns quickly, and only a small stub of wax remains as the flickering fire of the wick dances wildly. The wagon rocks back and forth, pulled slowly onward by the donkey that is all too happy to put as much distance between it and the skeletons that slowly follow after the companions as they move down the old road toward the mountain range that hangs like a dark, jagged set of teeth on the horizon.

Akori holds her staff protectively as her tails flick back and forth with a clear tension. *"They are still following."*

Thaco bristles. *"Well, if you have a magic candle, speak up because this was my last one."*

As you look back over the sea of skeletons, armed with jagged weapons and glinting armor, broken shields and tattered leather, you lose count before you even begin breaking one hundred heads. . . . They are endless and hungry. And no matter what you and your companions do, they are coming for you. . . .

Quest XII

Basing Your Miniatures

While we are on the subject of creating atmosphere and environment in your miniature hobby work, let's touch upon basing your models—how and why we do it—and examine some of the materials that can be used to help us along the way.

Once you have spent your time painting and perfecting your model, you'll likely notice that most miniatures are standing upon a circular, oval, or square base of some sort that helps to ensure that the figure can stand on a variety of surfaces.

While not a required step, many hobbyists discover that this tiny piece of used real estate offers an enormous opportunity to tell more of the story of the model and to help tether it into a world of your making.

Some of the simplest and most popular options include using fine-grain sand, static grass, and tufts of flocking to replicate vegetation and plant growth, soil, and earth of all types, colors, seasons, and styles.

Additionally, a good scenic base can include cork, slate tile, rocks, branches, resin or 3D-printed additions, and so much more. Personally, I have glued drinking straws, coffee stirs, beads and jewelry parts, and other such repurposed ephemera to create many diverse environments for my models.

In this Quest, I have documented a basic recipe for using some common items to base your first miniatures.

Using fine-grain sand or common dirt that has been collected from your front yard, use a thin application of PVA (basic white glue)—watered down a touch as needed—to the base, avoiding the feet of the model itself.

Apply a thin layer of your chosen material and allow it to dry fully and completely before moving on.

Once dry, coat the entire base in a dark brown wash and allow it to fully dry, encouraging it along with the gentle use of a hair dryer, if desired.

Next, take a lighter brown and use the dry-brushing technique to paint the higher texture of the sand, creating a strong contrast.

Using a little grass or flock, put a few small drops of thicker PVA on the base and apply your foliage and ground cover. Allow the glue to dry and spray the entire model with a little varnish.

The tavern, once much nicer than it is now, was built here to guard against the incursion of the creatures that once used these caverns to attack the nearby village. But years of neglect and at least a generation of dust have left it forgotten and lost. After another moment of consultation of the crusty old map, you find yourself tapping along the stone of the crumbling cellar wall in the hopes of some clue as to the location of the entrance.hjhh

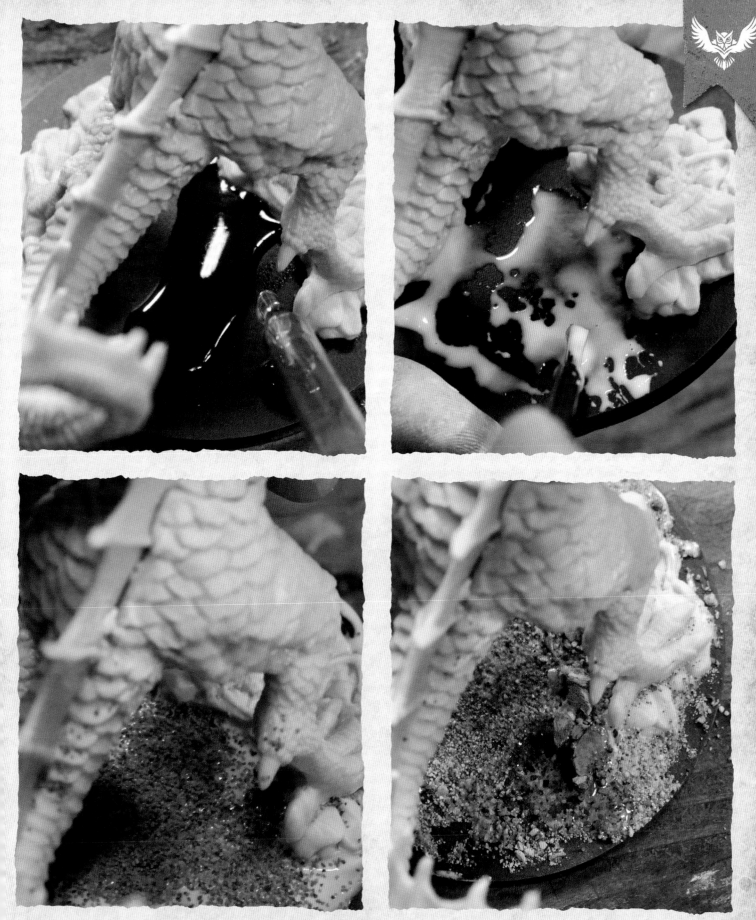

There are a wide variety of materials that may be used in the creation of a scenic base for your models. While sand and ballast are certainly the most popular, other creative options are easily acquired and used. One of my personal favorites is the use of cork. Cork comes in sheets at most craft and hobby stores, but you can salvage it from old bulletin boards and save a few pennies. The great thing about cork is that as it is broken, glued together, and painted, it makes for a lightweight, easy-to-use material to create rock-like steps and craggy groundworks. As a lightweight, porous material, cork can be easily glued together with a number of adhesives. Here I'm using superglue to tack the base pieces together and to create a pleasing shape upon which I can build. Once that is dry, I've added a healthy layer of black texture paint. This is one of my preferred, ready-made,

brands from Vallejo, but you can easily make your own using sand and acrylic paint. This coat is very thick and should be left overnight to thoroughly dry. After the texture paint is fully and completely dry, I over-brush a healthy coat of gray paint on the entire surface, not working too hard to obscure or cover the deepest recesses. I then dry brush the base with a variety of colors. For my money, good rock rendering comes with the careful use of warm and cool colors to add depth and visual interest. Study rocks in nature, and you'll see many layers and colors mingling together. While some rocks are completely gray, there is so much more variety and depth on display in your garden or backyard. Finally, using a little glue, I adhere some remade grass tufts to the base and prepare it for the miniature, which I glue on afterward.

Your knuckles rap against the cold stone, and your candle sputters before extinguishing as you pass a wall covered in rotten brooms and buckets. It was a gust of wind that did it.

A gust of wind . . . in the cellar?

With a fresh tinder twig, you light your candle once again and seat it in an old rusted lantern that you pull from the crumbling wall. Wind doesn't appear out of nowhere, and it serves to believe that this candle may be able to guide you in more ways than just providing light . . . With a small amount of exploration, you bring your candle close to the old stone wall and—sure as the suns rise—your candle is extinguished by the phantom breeze once more.

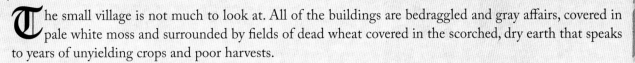

The small village is not much to look at. All of the buildings are bedraggled and gray affairs, covered in pale white moss and surrounded by fields of dead wheat covered in the scorched, dry earth that speaks to years of unyielding crops and poor harvests.

Of all of the cottages, only one or two of them seem to be occupied. In the creeping pink and orange light of the morning, it becomes clear that this small hamlet has been long forgotten and is rarely visited by outsiders.

Thaco Thistle-Britches scratches his chin and the tuft of purple hair that grows there. *"Hmmm. I thought that I had been to every tiny burg and outpost settlement from here to the Kingdom of Arcona, but I ain't never set foot in this town. Seems like they are under a bad omen. Those fields surely haven't produced more than dirt in three years."*

The orange-furred fox folk looks to the horizon and the looming mountain range silhouetted by the slowly lightening sky before turning back to the goblin merchant and you. Akori speaks softly, the truth of the situation slowly revealing itself to them as they discover it. *"The bad omen is named Thraddnirix, and he's a red dragon that is legend in these mountains."*

You look about as you see the marks upon the roofs of the cottages on the far end of the small village—the tops of them are all burnt and ruined. In the center of the town square, a large area of stone has been cleared, and claw marks the size of Thaco's wagon mar the ground.

The path that was shown to you by the Eye of Wonder is quite clear: follow the path to Hearthfire Mountain and ascend to the Tower of Mordaine, the only structure on that jagged peak . . . and home to a legendary red dragon. But first, mayhaps, you and your companions can try your luck at bartering for a little breakfast.

Quest

The Final Challenge - Thraddnirix
The Red - Airbrushing Monsters

Assembling and Painting Large Models and Monsters

While most of our work to this point has been on traditionally sized 28-mm figures, there are plenty of opportunities to undertake larger painting projects. Whether you set your sights upon a statuary bust, a piece of terrain, or something more monstrous, the lessons that we've explored will serve you just as well as they have on our more diminutive excursions.

That said, there are a few considerations in adjusting our efforts to larger projects. Within this Quest, we will review the necessary steps in assembling, preparing, and painting a larger model.

Additionally, we will delve deeper into the use of an airbrush, and while the use of that tool is not required to complete the Quest, the instruction does focus upon the speed and flexibility of that tool.

Should you decide to move forward without an airbrush, simply follow the previous Quests in priming and base coating our subject to get you caught up to the point that we begin to shade and highlight.

In this exercise I will be using an inexpensive and easily obtainable model from Reaper Miniatures. Reaper 77328 Cinder is the product SKU code, and you can find it on Reaper's website or at any number of online retailers. Conversely, you can always go to your friendly local gaming store and ask for them to order it for you, if, in fact, they do not have it in stock.

This model is a member of the Bones line of products and is very accessible in many ways. This is not a paid promotion; I simply feel strongly about the ease of use that this particular brand and style of miniature provides for a budding hobbyist. Even as an advanced miniature painter, I find myself picking up some items from the Reaper Bones line from time to time to paint and enjoy.

Aside from being inexpensive, these models are easy to assemble and paint.

If you would like to try another dragon, however, the steps included here are fully applicable and can be transferred to the great wyrm of your choice. The purpose of this exercise is to incorporate all of our previous Quests together in a large, exciting project that offers us the opportunity to hone our skills and experiment a bit on large surface areas.

Without further ado, let's
SLAY THIS BEAST. . . .

In preparing the model for assembly, we are going to clean up all of the parts with a sharp hobby knife. First, wash the model in a bath of warm water and a drop of soap and allow it to fully dry. Once assembled, we will utilize our newfound basing skills to create some texture with PVA glue, sand, and some small bits of cork and other debris to simulate large stones and rocks.

Cleaning up the model is more involved than with our previous miniatures. There is plenty of surface area to concern ourselves with, and we are working to isolate any regions of flash and mold lines. We gently scrape away any blemishes and glue the model together using superglue. I also used a bit of Milliput—epoxy putty—to fill in the gaps around the wings and other areas that needed a little transition between the parts of the model. This stage isn't essential but helps to eliminate any cracks and fissures that make the model feel less than complete.

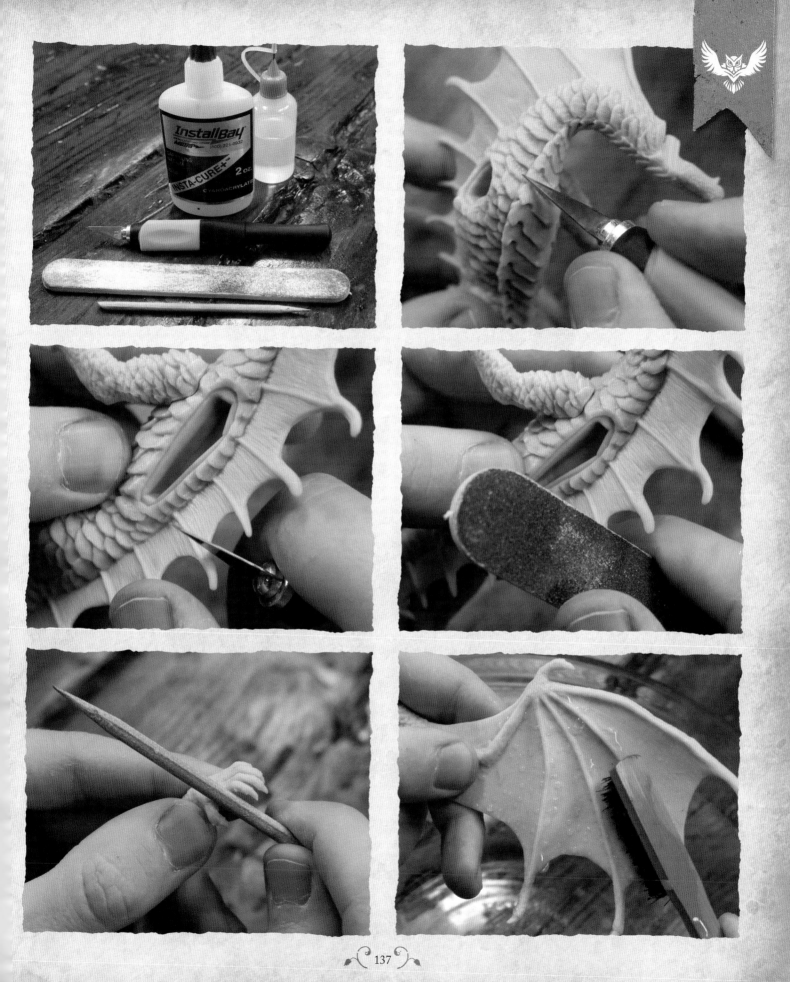

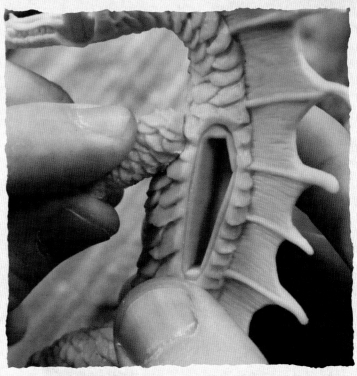

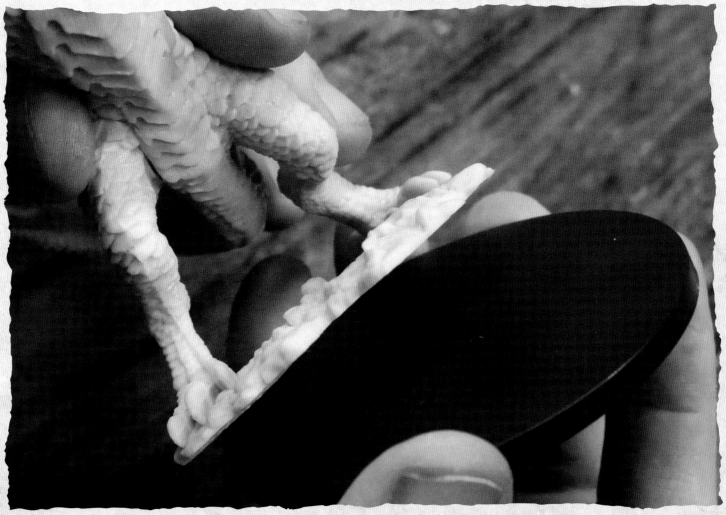

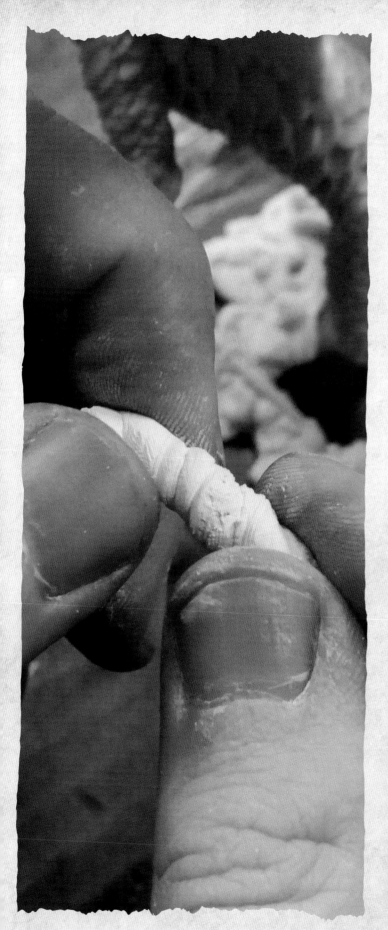

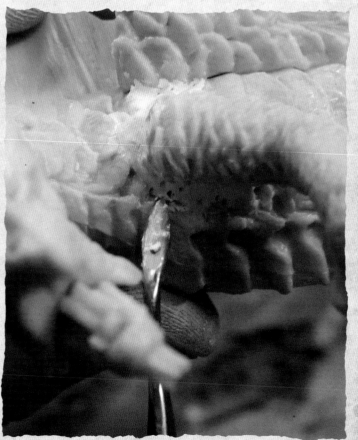

When all of the preparation work is finished, I prepare a thinned mixture of black primer paint and apply it over the entire model in a series of even and thin coats. Two or three passes served me well in this example. Remember that with the airbrush, the best results are acquired when you are working with material that is correctly prepared. Judge the thickness of your paint carefully and work in even, thin coats. After the black has dried, I applied a gray zenithal spray effect from the angle that I felt best suited my imagined light source.

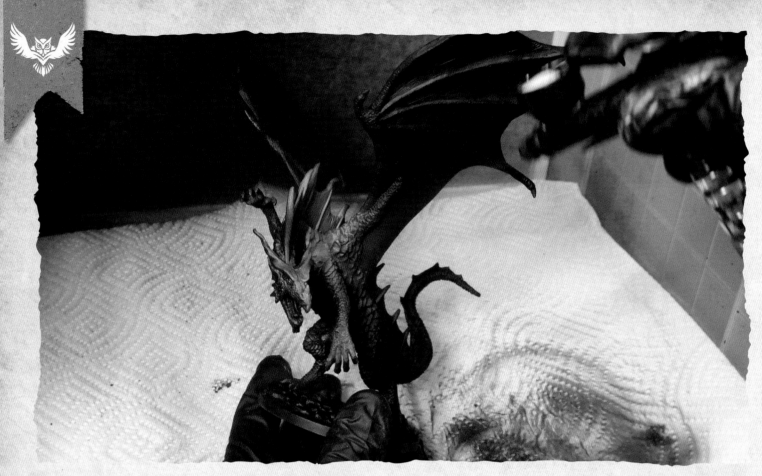

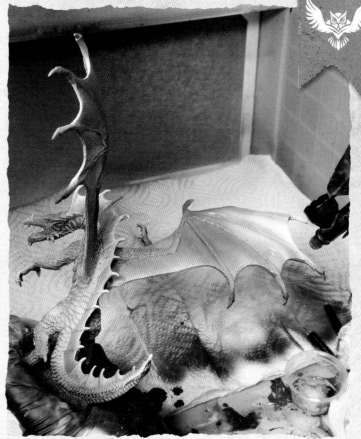

After the undercoat and primer have fully dried, I load my airbrush up with some yellow ink. Again, the use of ink in this context is a powerful tool to introduce bright hues without obscuring the shadows and highlights that we created with our black and gray undercoat. Working my way up, and not bothering to clean out the cup of my airbrush, I introduce orange and red onto the model, focusing on the body and deeper recesses. You could use any combination of colors in this way.

As with our earlier adventures, I have mixed up an oil wash here with the same mix of mineral spirits and dark oil paint. I mixed a little black and a little crimson together to create a shade that accentuates the red and orange on the model. Again, these colors are a matter of choice, and the process can be altered as you see fit to help you achieve the dragon of your dreams.

Applying a careful oil wash over the scales and texture portions of the dragon, we are significantly darkening the model, but, as before, we will be using mineral spirits on a tightly packed cotton swab or with a synthetic brush to carefully remove any unwanted material. After letting the wash dry overnight, I then seal the entire model with matte varnish. Once that is fully dry, the real fun begins. . . .

With the varnish coat dry and the figure in a good place, we can begin to do the work of painting and improving on the natural highlights and shadows that the earlier steps have provided us. Here, I am mixing together a few paints to create some colors to use in deepening the shadows, altering the vibrancy of some areas, and adding details and effects along the length of the dragon.

The shade will work itself into the deepest recesses and quickly and efficiently create strong definition and contrast. The great thing about oil washes is that they take a long time to dry, allowing you plenty of freedom to remove and manipulate

your work. Oils can be a powerful and dynamic tool, despite their complications.

When working with a model of any size, as we've discussed elsewhere in this tome, we should always consider the light source and how it is affecting the subject. Where is the light coming from, and what sort of secondary light source might be affecting the colors of the model? Here I am using a number of blues and purples to create a strong contrast against the reds, oranges, and yellows.

Painting the details such as the eyes, teeth, and horns allows us a quick means to ground the strong elements of the model that we have undertaken already. Again, I'm using desaturated tones to create a striking visual focus. The lighter off-white of the horns helps to draw your focus to the face. As lovely as the wings are going to be once we are finished, the face is the most expressive portion of the model.

With a very thin red-purple glaze, I have begun to work in freehand-painted veins on the wings. Freehand painting is the addition of an element that is not present on the sculpture of the model but is rather added in the painting process using your skill and imagination. Such brushwork is easy to grasp and can lead to even more ambitious work in the future—banners, tattoos, embroidery, and more! The base is also cleaned up at this point.

Outside of painting the rim of the base, other basic cleanup on the model will serve us well at this stage. I am touching up the highest points on the model with a mixture that is approaching a purer—but never really pure—white. This helps to create some visual pop on the teeth and horns. Even a little glint in the eye is far less intimidating on a model of this size, and you might feel ready to give it a try.

Highlighting is crucial when playing with the translucent qualities of something like the membranes of a dragon's wings. I worked on these wings over the course of an hour or so, building up yellows and deepening the purples in certain areas. By leaving the center as bright and light as possible and blending down into the purple shadows, I was able to achieve this effect.

Careful consideration as to the lighting and color selection is important in undertaking any miniature project. Remember to ask yourself the questions that help to determine the story that lies within your artwork. All of these tools are yours to weld, and with practice, the possibilities of what you can render are limitless.

The blazing fire stretches as far as the eye can see; the entire mountainside of the Hearthfire Mountain is burning. After three days of exploration in the ruined Tower of Moridaine, you and your companions have finally found the amulet held by that beastly troll.

The minion of Thraddnirix the Red is not eager to relinquish his treasure, and in the battle that ensues, both you and Thaco are badly injured. The dragon lies in a cavern beneath the tower, but the only way to safely access that lair is through a magical gateway—a gateway that requires the golden amulet in your bleeding hand. But once the troll has been slain, the dragon bursts free from his horde under the mountain and covers the entire mountain with fire.

There is no easy way of retreat, and while the beast could fly in and out of its cavern from the grand fissure at the top of the mountain, you and your companions require more terrestrial means of entry.

Akori is already tethering a rope about their waist, and all nine of their tails are swishing back and forth in anticipation of the jump ahead of them. With a heavy sigh, knowing that you have come too far to give up, you grab onto the rope and look to Thaco. *"Nothing in that last pack is going to get us out of this situation easily, eh?"*

With a crooked grin, the goblin smiles up at you. *"Nope. And I don't offer refunds, exchanges, or apologies. All sales are final."*

You descend into the lair of the great red dragon, quite different from the person who set out from the tavern all of those weeks back. You are wiser, more experienced, and ready to face the unknown. . . .

What is an ending but the start of something else?

I hope that *Arcane Arts* has been entertaining to read, informative and enjoyable to paint alongside, and—hopefully—encouraging. Miniature painting and crafting are lifelong joys of mine, and if I have done you any service in this writing, then you are excited to explore it more fully.

There are endless paths in art, and this book has been just one. Never stop learning and reading and seeking new pathways.

The best part of any hobby and craft is that your skill will improve the more time that you spend honing it, and that journey is your own. Take your time or hurry up—the choice is yours. Just keep making things, sharing ideas, building, painting, and enjoying yourself!

If you want to find me, you can. I'm easily accessible online and often paint on my personal Twitch channel, twitch.tv/scabbyrooster. Come ask me questions or chat with others who enjoy painting as well. The tavern is always open, and all of my hobby work takes place in the Broom Closet. You'll find me there.

If you wish to acquire the exact models used in this book, you need only use the links included here. HeroForge is a wonderful tool, and their service is available at heroforge.com

At the end of it all, if you leave this book with a single lesson, please take this with you: There are endless worlds waiting to be given form by your hand, countless stories waiting to be told, and unimagined wonders that you are yet to create. Don't waste any time, make some magic, and never, ever stop.

Guide Hall Map

The Adventurer's Guild

The Hero's Rest - Guides to Painting and Hobby Equipment

Throughout our adventures together, I have mentioned—time and time again—that there are some very special sections of wayward information contained within the book that are awaiting you and ready for your perusal when the time comes. Well, within this final section, those scattered bits and stray thoughts await you. They are not as fulsome as some of the other portions of this manual and are meant to guide you on to further exploration outside of the confines of these pages. I hope that they lead you in the right direction and help to open new possibilities in your hobby journey.

Lastly, you'll find some QR codes that will allow you to visit the Discord and interact directly with myself and other hobbyists, ask questions, and share your own work and progress.

P1—The Painting Portfolios

There are many brands of paint within the hobby modeling world, and the choices available to a new modeler are more numerous and diverse than ever before. In fact, the sheer quantity of choices can become overwhelming. To assist you in selecting the material that is right for you, I have created very brief portfolios that—clearly and honestly—give you my personal opinion on the strengths and weaknesses of some of the more readily available brands of paint that can be found on the market today.

Again, these are simply my opinions, and I encourage you to use my advice or explore on your own and make your own determinations. Also, while I include a healthy selection of brands here, I promise you that I will have overlooked a particular paint line or two, and that should in no way be taken as a determination of quality or worth. That said, let's talk paint.

Vallejo—Vallejo has a wide range of paints with its various lines and most are affordably priced and of high quality. The Model Color line is readily available at a number of bigger box retail stores in the United States and can't be beaten for accessibility and cost. They are matte and opaque with good coverage and can be thinned with water nicely. Additionally, the Metal Color line is my personal favorite true metallic paint choice! Vallejo is always my first recommendation to brand-new painters, as there are a wide variety of paint sets that cover all of the bases without a huge investment.

Reaper—Reaper's Core Colors line is another of my first recommendations and a mainstay in my personal hobby work. The highly pigmented paints within their offerings flow well and rarely require much thinning or manipulation before application. The Reaper crew are enormously talented and personable, and you are likely never going to find better customer service or personal attention elsewhere. This company is based in the United States and takes great care in the quality of their product, with their paint lines being mixed by only one or two individuals to ensure consistency and quality. The Learn to Paint – Core Skills box is a perfect place to start, as it includes paints, brushes, instruction booklets, and miniatures for a very reasonable price.

Citadel Colour—The big dogs of the miniature wargaming scene have been providing paint since the very beginnings of the hobby, and I have many fond memories of my first painting excursions with some of the old box sets that Games Workshop used to put out. It was a simpler time, and Goblin Green was about one of twenty colors of paint available on any hobby shop shelf outside of the Ral Partha line. Most of my friends and I made the mistake of using hobby car enamels to try and paint our models, and Citadel was the first to step in and show us the error of our ways.

Nostalgia aside, Games Workshop has evolved and still produces some of the best paints on the market. They also still use the same basic style of paint pot that they have used since they first bottled paints. This means that Citadel paint tends to spill and dry out if not carefully handled and protected. Worse,

it costs way more than other paints of similar quality. The Contrast line, some of the Technical and Texture options, and the Shades are all worth the price and are specialized enough to make analogs few and far between but—truth be told—I don't feel that any new hobbyist should feel obligated to march the Citadel path. Pick out what you really like from the Citadel line and, perhaps, save your money by choosing a different paint line for your workhorse colors.

Monument Hobbies—The Pro Acryl line from Monument Hobbies is a newer tool in my painting arsenal, but I couldn't be happier with the results. These affordable and generously sized paint bottles come with the best dispenser in the field, and the wide variety of pigments are strong and easy to use. They mix easily and dry matte. The Translucent line is the best remade glazing product available in my humble opinion, and the small business ethos and care that Monument Hobbies embodies are apparent in their great customer service.

Scale 75—Scale Color is the painters' paint line, meaning that it is the paint line that I feel I hear advanced painters taking about the most. Note that I didn't say ALL advanced painters, just the ones that I hang around. This paint is different in a lot of ways and is a gel-based medium that can be very difficult to work with if you are not used to the differences in thinning and manipulating the materials. The Kimera line is one of my favorites, with deeply rich and intense pigments that can be thinned and cut down for days and days without separation. And the Artist series is a thick, creamy acrylic that I use often and recommend to those that are used to working with traditional artist paints. If you are seeking to mix your own colors and want to explore three or four color schemes, mixing with the Artist series is one of my personal choices. In short, I don't recommend these paints to beginning painters due to the complicated nature of the application, but I strongly recommend them to those looking to improve their work after spending a good amount of time working with some of the more approachable brands.

Army Painter—While I admittedly have the least experience with their regular paint line, I use their colored spray primers, dips, and washes quite regularly. While airbrushing can be a wonderful way to apply primer and base coats, the Army painter line of rattle-can spray primers is amazing and produces quick, easy results that can make your army painting projects much more approachable. If you have a pile of skeletons to prepare for a roleplaying session, try their spray and dip approach. You would be hard-pressed to find a more efficient way to get speedy results.

Cuttlefish Colors—Cephalopod Studios is a small, boutique-style paint maker that offers some of the absolute best neon paints available anywhere. They do a wonderful job of creating unique and interesting hues that aren't readily available elsewhere, and they have found a nice niche within the hobby space.

Badger—As a completely airbrush focused line, Badger paints may not have much utility to you, but if you are an avid airbrush user, then the Minitaire range is easily one of the most affordable and easy-to-use products that I own in my personal hobby storehouse.

Mig Jimenez – Ammo—This specialty paint line is adored by model vehicle and diorama painters, and it has so much to offer in the hobby gaming space. Streaking grimes and aging materials are becoming more and more common, but this is my personal favorite line for easy and quick applications of realistic mud, grease, and goop.

Tamiya—Offering wonderful translucent colors of intense vibrancy, the Tamiya acrylic line has some real powerhouses if you are looking to accent your traditional acrylics with gems, metallic shading, or specialized gloss coats. I highly recommend their reds, greens, and yellows if you are seeking to mix up blood and gore for something gruesome.

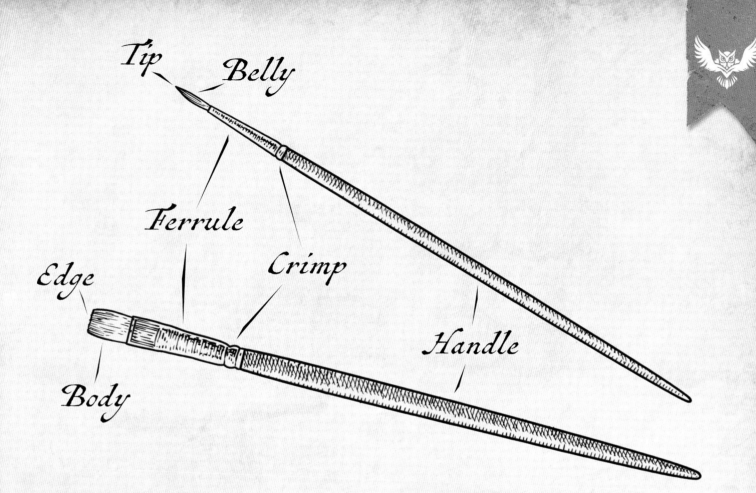

B1—The Way Of The Brush

A listing of brushes and the methods with which to care for them. Washing and cleaning brushes.

The best brushes for the hobby are typically sable hair, as the natural qualities of the organic bristles give the brush more desirable qualities than synthetic brushes. Your brush should hold but not absorb the material and bend and flex as you work. Also, durability is crucial.

There are various sizes and measurements throughout all of the many brush lines. The Winsor & Newton Series 7 number 2 is a popular choice, but it isn't a cheap one. This brush is a good baseline for seeking out a quality instrument. Smaller and larger brushes have been used in hobby work, and synthetics are important whenever you are working with enamels or performing harsh tasks that you wish to spare your expensive sable hairbrushes from enduring. The Army Painter offers a great starter set of three brushes for a very reasonable price. Most importantly, always clean and condition your brushes after each and every hobby session. Using warm water and a brush shop like The Masters, thoroughly clean the brush and allow it dry without damaging the tip of the brush or putting undo water into the ferrule.

B2—The Anotomy Of A Brush

Every brush is comprised of some basic parts, and knowing them will aid you in getting the most out of your work.

The TIP is just that. The very point of a brush. On flat brushes, this end is called an EDGE.

The BELLY is the large portion of brush that holds the majority of your material, be it paint or ink or wash. On a flat brush, this is called a BODY, but the principle is the same.

The FERRULE is the metal collar that binds the bristles of the brush together and holds them to the handle.

The CRIMP is the point of connection between the FERRULE and the HANDLE

The HANDLE is the wooden, plastic, or metal rod that allows for the artist to grip the tool.

B3—Cleaning and Caring For Your Brushes

Proper brush maintenance and care can prolong the life of your brushes and help you to produce better work as you are not fighting against the problems that a damaged paintbrush can create when painting a model. The steps are simple, and the materials are widely available.

Soap and Warm Water—While there are plenty of professional brands of soap that you can use on your brushes, I find that anything that you would use to wash your hands is perfectly acceptable. Brush bristles—especially expensive sable hairbrushes—are much like human hair and should be treated with a gentle hand.

Warm water is important, and you don't want to use water that is too hot and melt or unbind any glue that might be holding the bristles together.

Carefully dry your brushes and reshape the tips by gently twirling them between your fingers or on the palm of the hand.

If you need it, due to stray bristles that are splaying away from the body of the brush, use a little brush conditioner or reshaper to bring the brush back to a sharp point.

Leaving brushes in your water pot to soak can cause a myriad of problems and damage them after continued misuse. Inside the ferrule of a brush, the bristles are bound together using an adhesive glue that can be weakened with time. This wear and tear will cause flyaway bristles and misalign the tip of your brush.

Certainly never leave your brush in the water with the bristles pressing down into the bottom of the water pot, as this will quickly leave kinks and bends in your brush that won't easily be teased out.

The best practice is to keep your brush wet as you work to prevent paint from becoming trapped in the ferrule but to avoid prolonged soaking. Use a brush soap and shaper or conditioner and store your brushes lying on their sides or pointed straight up into the air, upside down in a container.

C1—Character Questionnaires

If you are seeking to expand the story of your characters, to discover more about the miniature that you've decided to paint, but are hitting a wall in terms of sussing out the who, why, how, and particulars about your subject, you can find a wild array of resources that will help you to answer those questions. Below are some questions that you might want to ask.

Describe your character's current appearance.

What would most people think when they first see your character?

What deity, if any, does your character worship?

What is your character's opinion on nobility? On authority?

Has your character ever been in love?

Does your character regret any particular choice that they have made?

What would your character say their best trait would be?

What is your character's greatest fear?

What are your character's hobbies and interests?

What is your character the most insecure about?

What person does your character admire most?

If your character had time to pick up any artisan's tools, game set, instrument, etc., what would it be?

What is your character's current goal?

Does your character ever want to "settle down"?

If your character wasn't an adventurer, what livelihood would they lead?

Who would your character trust the most with their life?

What are your character's core moral beliefs?

What relationship does your character have with their parents and siblings?

What item that your character has collected during the adventure is the most important to them?

Is there any particular weapon, item, etc., that your character longs to find?

Where does your character feel the most at home?

Does your character care about how they're perceived by others? How do they change themselves to fit in with other people?

What does your character think is the true meaning of life?

What is your character's scent?

How does your character feel about receiving/giving orders? Are they more of a leader or follower?

With a small amount of exploration, you bring your candle close to the old stone wall and—sure as the suns rise—your candle is extinguished by the phantom breeze once more.

After the use of your third to last tinder twig, you light your candle and put it back into the old rusty lantern. You can now see that the dust hasn't settled in the recesses of the big roughhewn stones about five feet from the packed dirt floor.

What does your character's name represent to them?

Is your character more of an introvert or an extrovert?
What does your character want to be remembered by?

Does your character consider themselves a hero, villain, or something else?

Where does your character see themselves in 20 years?

What is your character's relationship with magic?

How did your character spend their childhood?

What aspect of your character's future are they most curious about?

What colors are associated with your character?

If your character was granted a single use of Wish, what would they use it for?

What type of creature in the world is your character the most intrigued by?

When they were a child, what did your character want to be or think they were going to be when they grew up?

What is your character's greatest achievement?

Is your character willing to risk the well-being of others in order to achieve their goal?

What is your character's favorite food?

How generous is your character?

What is your character's biggest pet peeve?

What memory does your character want to forget the most?

Who is your character's biggest rival?

What is your character's guiltiest pleasure?

What is your character's biggest flaw?

How did your character learn the languages that they speak?

What is most important to your character: health, wealth, or happiness?

What advice would your character give to a younger version of themselves?

What, currently, is your character the most curious about?

What is your character's favorite season?

What animal best represents your character?

Setting your pack and the lantern aside, you rub your cold hands together and place them firmly on the stone wall and push heavily, leaning your shoulder and back into it.

The very cumbersome and heavy wall slides inward, and—not expecting the ease of the task— you are thrust forward into a mass of thick spiderwebs and musty air.

How long have you wandered these passages?

It seems as if you've been walking for hours, journeying through the winding twists and turns of the Kobold Caverns. The map has saved you some searching, and your lantern continues to burn, for the moment, but the deeper you go and the farther from the tavern cellar that you delve, the less certain that you are that you could easily return to the relative safety of the seedy inn.

D1–D3—Dimensional Magicks

There are many things that can be said about the technological improvements that 3D printing have undergone over the recent years, and while I could fill another book this size with details and thoughts on the subject, I have included just the most bare of overviews here.

D1—Types Of 3d Printing

For hobby 3D printing, you'll almost always use one of the two following types of printing, either resin—which offers high detailed models but considerably more mess and potential danger—of filament printing which isn't as details and difficult to calibrate.

1. Stereolithography (SLA)
   - https://3dinsider.com/3d-printer-types/#sla

2. Fused deposition Modeling (FDM)
   - https://3dinsider.com/3d-printer-types/#fdm

D2—Where to Learn More

   http://www.fatdragongames.com
   https://www.3dprintedtabletop.com

D3—Printing and Ordering Miniatures

Within this section, there are a number of helpful links and QR codes that you can follow to purchase physical miniatures to match those used in this book or download the digital files to print them all on an FDM (filament printers) or resin 3D printer.

R1–R3—Arcane Academy

R1—Color Theory

Color theory is the practical combination of our understanding of how colors compliment and contrast each other. An ancient wizard known as Isaac Newton is—to the best of our knowledge—the first to have mapped the color spectrum in a circular form. The relationship between colors can be divined through the use of a color wheel, many examples of which have been included here in this tome for you to utilize in the work that you will undertake in choosing the schemes for your models.

I recommend that you explore a variety of readily available resources on the subject, such as color wheels and traditional art books, but I suggest that you examine some of the fulsome sites that have been created to allow you to test and explore a variety of color theory combination. My favorite is listed below:

   https://www.canva.com/colors/color-wheel/

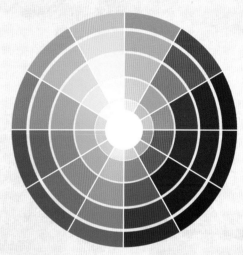

R2—Inspiration

There are countless ways to collect and build mood boards and to collect images that you can use for reference in painting your models. While learning from other painted work is a wonderful tool, you would do well to also go back to the source and seek out solid images of the material in question. Obviously the Inter-webs will serve you well in this endeavor; however, I personally prefer to use Pinterest boards to organize my references into neatly wrapped files, labeled and stored for when they are needed in one place.

   https://www.pinterest.com

R3—Free Dice Apps

If you're looking for a free dice app, look no further than Dice Roller for Apple users or Prime Dice for Android Users.

W1—World Building

If you are seeking to tell more stories using your hobby miniature work, why not document your progress and share it in a community of like-minded individuals? The Discord linked in the QR codes will have special sections that are devoted to the exploration of themes and ideas that are expressed in the work of artists and hobbyists just like you! If you want to read up on ways to elaborate on your work, *On Writing and World-building* by Timothy Hickson is a good reference.

You can find any number of tutorials that will instruct you on the basics of painting models and miniatures, converting, and kitbashing—and I'm thankful for it—but I feel that the discussion and exploration of the more academic elements of color usage and storytelling are often missing. That's why this book is in your hands.

This discussion is the root—and the quickest way—to improve the results of your work. Understanding some of the classic "art room" education will give you the confidence to make more informed choices and focus the results of your storytelling.

Glossary

Complementary Color Combinations—When we are seeking the most pronounced contrast and impact between colors, we look to the opposite side of the color wheel to pair a color with a partner that will generate a bright and elevated synergy between the two.

Monochromatic Scheme—Using a number of tones, shades, and tints of the same hue, we create a more harmonious and unified palette that can allow more subtle results than those that are created through complementary combinations. We'll examine the specific reasons and uses of this sort of choice further in our adventures.

Analogous Color Combinations—These are three colors that are adjacent to each other on the color wheel. These combinations create an ease of use that is both harmonious and pleasing. They are safe and stable together, leaving the sharp contrasts of other combinations aside.

Airbrushing

PSI—Pounds per square inch; a measure of pressure within your compressor. An air compressor uses a tank and compresses the air to create pressure that, when released, propels through the tubes of your rig and through the tip of your airbrush.

Piles of Shame—Unpainted models that sit in their boxes unused, typically while you find excuses to purchase additional models to build and paint.

WHY HAVE YOU FORSAKEN US?!

Voiding—When a painter cleans the paint off of their brush quickly so that they can use it to blend wet paint on a model without adding more paint. Often painters will lick the small amount of paint off of their brush, which leads to eating the paint and adds to the brush a small amount of saliva, which is slightly more viscous than water and used in blending. It is not recommended and is seen as a dark art by some who witness it.

Two-Brush Blending—A more socially acceptable manner with which to achieve similar results to "voiding" but requires some practice, as the painter is wielding two separate brushes at the same time.

Layer Painting—Stacking layers of paint on top of each other to achieve the illusion of light striking a model. Oftentimes, the paint is of a similar hue and darker in the recesses while building up successively lighter "layers" of paint.

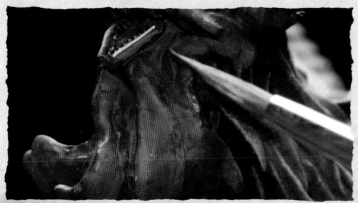

Edge Highlighting—Painting just the very edge of a model, at various points, to create separation and imitate the highlight of illumination at the sharpest edges of an object.

Dry Brushing—A technique that utilizes a brush, heavily saturated in paint, that is wiped mostly clean before it is scrubbed along the surface of a model to create texture and definition by quickly producing highlights.

Zenithal Priming—The use of a dark primer coat, followed by a lighter coat of paint or ink, to build an instant rendering of light upon the model. This technique is often used in conjunction with thin ink coats and other processes that allow the dark and light underpainting to remain visible on the model.

Online Resources and Suggested Creators

Here is the short list of some of the most instructive and entertaining content creators in the world of miniature painting and hobby. This is, of course, based on the creators I am personally familiar with, and I'm absolutely certain that I've missed a phenomenal artist and creator—most likely more than a few.

Please forgive me for any exclusion and feel free to join us in the comment sections of our Discord community and share them with us. Those links are included in this section along with a QR code for easy use.

Sam Lenz – Twitch – https://www.twitch.tv/samsonarts

Shoshie's Painting – Twitch – https://www.twitch.tv/ShoshiesMinis

Jimmy the Brush – Twitch – https://www.twitch.tv/jimmythebrush

BrushforHire – Twitch – https://www.twitch.tv/brushforhire

Dana Howl – YouTube – https://www.youtube.com/c/DanaHowl

Slowfuse_Monument - Twitch - https://www.twitch.tv/monument_slowfuse

Miniac – YouTube – https://www.youtube.com/c/Miniac

GooberTown Hobbies – YouTube – https://www.youtube.com/c/GoobertownHobbies

JLM – YouTube – https://www.youtube.com/channel/UCG7ErJtvi7Z4OiXSuAeKdZg

Cult of Paint – YouTube – https://www.youtube.com/channel/UCPI4wJgB2hlWZqz0tRqg4qQ

Dallas Kemp - YouTube – https://www.youtube.com/watch?v=XAq23uPG31o

The Mini Witch – https://www.youtube.com/c/LylaMev

Sorastro – https://www.youtube.com/c/Sorastro

Squidmar – https://www.youtube.com/c/SquidmarMiniatures

Doctor Faust – https://www.youtube.com/c/ThePaintingClinic

Zumikito – https://www.youtube.com/c/Zumikito

Reaper Miniatures – https://www.reapermini.com

Inkarnate – https://inkarnate.com

The Scabby Rooster Tavern Twitch channel is my personal venue for gaming and hobby-related content, as well as the Arcane Arts YouTube channel, where you can find a plethora of tutorials and videos that will help guide you further into the world of hobby painting and game-play. Feel free to find me there or on Instagram and Twitter @eatenbypotchky. I'd be happy to help you in any way possible; join me for a Twitch painting session, leave a comment on Youtube, or find me on the Discord server!

HeroForge is an amazing online resource for you to use in designing, creating, and producing your own unique models. You can use their powerful 3D rendering tools to design color schemes, create digital assets to use in a Virtual TableTop software, or buy professionally printed 3D models of your creations to paint. The wizards at HeroForge have been kind enough to allow me to utilize their tools to design and print the models that I've used in this manual, and—if you are interested—you can use the QR code below to access their website and print out the exact model designs that I've used here.